Strong Finish

Your Life Today is Your Legacy Tomorrow

By
Michael S. Miller

E-BookTime, LLC
Montgomery, Alabama

Strong Finish
Your Life Today is Your Legacy Tomorrow

ISBN: 978-1-60862-267-2

First Edition
Published March 2011
E-BookTime, LLC
6598 Pumpkin Road
Montgomery, AL 36108
www.e-booktime.com

Strong Finish

Dedication

I dedicate this book to my son, Michael.
Your "strong finish" is an inspiration to me.

Contents

Foreword
by Joe Eriquez

> *Everyone thinks of changing the world, but no one thinks of changing himself.* ~Leo Nikolaevich Tolstoy

I have known Mike Miller now for just over six years, and in that amount of time, I have had the privilege of watching the Lord work in his life. Over the years of getting to know Mike, I have listened to his story, from his childhood, his first marriage, losing his precious daughter in a car accident, to his time in the military, and to his present-day life as a successful businessman and family man.

Mike and I were sitting in a restaurant one day as he started to share his life with me. I watched as the tears rolled down the cheeks of this strong and proud combat veteran as his life unfolded in front of me. Starting with his childhood and moving into his teenage and adult years, his life was filled with one hardship after another. Mike was confused, angry, and bitter, but he just did not know how to let it go.

Mike was drawn to the U.S. Army where he became an exceptional soldier. He entered active duty as a Private E-1 (the lowest possible rank), graduated from Officer Candidate School five years later, and was excelling quickly. He was on the fast track to becoming a high-ranking officer. During his time of service, Mike was in the first Gulf War, and to this day, he has nightmares over the things he witnessed. The main reason he excelled was because he would not give an order that he himself would not perform. Mike led by example from the front; not just by title. It was more important to Mike for his soldiers to respect the man more than the rank. The military life suited him, and Mike understood the boundaries. It had direction, and most of all, the military gave him purpose. Mike was searching for purpose and anything that proved that his life mattered. All the things Mike did not receive growing up – approval, purpose, direction, and results – he received from the Army.

A few short months after joining the military, Mike was married to his high school sweetheart. They were blessed with two beautiful children – a boy and a girl. From the outside looking in, their marriage seemed to be perfect. In his effort to achieve professional success, he placed his family second. He volunteered for all the tough assignments, which kept him away from home. When he was home, he worked long hours and rarely saw his family. He thought being a good provider would make him a good husband and dad. He had become a good soldier and a good family man, so he thought. However, after nine years, the marriage was over. He had failed and had only himself to blame. This was his first major failure as an adult. He still struggles with the guilt.

Mike stayed in the Army, and shortly after his divorce, was one of ten Army Officers to attend a prestigious Marine Corps school. Despite his failed marriage, he continued to drive towards success. Unfortunately, Mike's health would not allow him to pursue his military career any longer. His knees had given out, and his field days were over. Mike's fast track to becoming a high-ranking officer was slipping away. I could see the hurt in Mike's eyes as he spoke of the emotional pain he felt. He had found something he was good at, and once again he had failed. This was his second major failure, and it came within 18 months of his divorce.

Shortly after leaving the Army, Mike took a job at the Pentagon. Here, he excelled again, and his life seemed to be turning around. During the 9/11 terrorist attacks, Mike was only a few blocks away from the plane that hit the Pentagon. Mike enjoyed his work. It was rewarding to be recognized by high-ranking military officers who leaned upon him for major decisions. Then he got the call that turned his world upside down. I will leave the details out, as they are shared in the chapters ahead.

The hurt, anger, and disappointment were building up in Mike's life. He seemed to have no peace, and God was very distant, rigid, and lifeless in the manner Mike understood Him. Mike was feeling like a failure. His life, from childhood to adulthood, was filled with one disappointment after another.

The next two years of Mike's life were filled with anger and bitterness that had reached an all-time high. He was at the point in his life where he cared very little about anything or anybody. He turned to drugs (prescription and illegal) and alcohol to try to numb the pain. Mike's choices were poor, and he was on the road to self-destruction. Although he leaves out the details of these two years, the pain on his face and the regret in his eyes tell more of the story than his lips ever could tell. For the first time in his life, he just wanted to give up. The fighter in him was ready to throw in the towel. His self-pity led him to believe there was nothing to live for.

He was wrong. He had two reasons to live. One reason had always been there, and the other reason was on the horizon.

His first reason for wanting to live was his son, Mike Jr. When Mike speaks of his son, the frown turns into a smile. He gets a glisten in his eye. Through all his mistakes, the one thing that has been consistent is Mike Jr.'s love for his dad. When he had been knocked down and ready to throw in the towel, it was his son that gave him strength to get up one more time.

The second reason to not give into defeat was the day he met Lisa. On a trip to Phoenix with Mike Jr., he met her and her two boys. Every other weekend, Lisa would fly to Washington, DC, or Mike would fly to Phoenix so they could see each other. It only took a few months before Mike knew he had found someone he could not live without. Less than a year from meeting, Mike moved to Phoenix and married Lisa. He looks back now and realizes that she played a major role in saving his life.

Finding Lisa allowed Mike to love another person again. This was a scary place for him, because in his career, there was direction, purpose, and disciplines he understood. In a marriage, there were none of these directives. He placed his feelings and faith in someone else and hoped it would work. Mike was driven to succeed in his new marriage and in his new career. His life seemed to be turning around. He started his own company, and in a short amount of time, became successful. Mike's drive and fortitude is what has made his company the success that it is.

Mike was now in a good marriage, and his career was more than he could imagine, but he still had a problem. The anger and bitterness that Mike had developed through the years was still present in his life. Though on the outside things looked well, Mike was still very empty inside. The next few steps in Mike's life would introduce a new fear. He would have to start to allow God to remove the dysfunction of anger and bitterness. What was hard to accept was these were the emotions that drove him to succeed. Sitting in that restaurant, I will never forget his words, "Joe, I do not know how to turn these things over to God. I am not even sure if I want to. This is how I have survived. This is how I have overcome the adversity in my life." Mike was finding out that you cannot be defined in the things you have or how successful a business might be, but only in the peace that comes from God.

Mike's journey would take him to a place that would challenge him to trust God. Trusting God was foreign ground. Mike would face one of the most significant challenges in his life – a war that is not fought on the traditional battle grounds, but within a man's heart and soul. The war was against all the issues he ran from – faith, trust, and true intimacy.

Today, God is alive in Mike's life. What does that mean? He still has his struggles, but we all do. The only difference now is Mike is not running from them. Even though his heart has softened and he has found new peace, he never lost his fighting spirit. He has learned to face the issues that ruled his life, but they are no longer his god. Mike has come to grips with the fact that, in life, bad things happen to good people, but God is still in control. Mike has seen God's truth work. He knows that God will take the bad and negative things that happen to us and turn them around and help us grow. In this spiritual growth, Mike has found out that life is not just about us individually, but also about how we can help each other through our tragedies. It is through this revelation that "Strong Finish" is birthed. Mike's desire is to share the stories of good people that have had bad things happen to them, but have triumphed victorious on the other side. He believes that if this book helps just one person, then every tear and every sleepless night was worth it.

Preface

Joe is my mentor and my friend. He has counseled me for a while and recommended that I write a book. I needed to forgive and allow God to give me peace. He truly believed that writing a book, or even a journal, would start the healing process. He saw the healing I experienced from writing "Maci's Place – The Loss of a Child Through a Father's Eyes." However, I knew that some of the things I would write about would hurt the feelings of others – specifically my mom. I wrestled for months with the decision, but finally decided to do it. However, prior to beginning, I wanted my mom to know. For those who know me, although I speak for a living, I find it very challenging to put my emotions into words. So, when I need to share my feelings, I normally write. Here is the email I sent mom:

Mom,

I wanted to write you a letter, but I thought an email would be better because you can actually keep it on your computer and do not have to worry about losing it. Anyways, I just wanted to share some things with you. I know it may seem impersonal, but I find that I can share my feelings much better on paper than when speaking. It's amazing how I can get in front of a thousand people and speak, but have trouble with the one-on-one. Anyways, it is what it is, right?

This year, I have really been going through some rough times emotionally. From the outside looking in, it probably seems like I have a good life. But on the inside, I am an emotional wreck. God has been working on my heart, and I have been fighting it all the way. I have been seeking counsel through Joe, and it has been very helpful. I think I kind of reached my culmination point with the Africa trip. A couple of days before we left, I talked to Joe. The passage he spoke was simple, but powerful – "Be still and know that I am God." Joe told me this was my opportunity to be away from my normal busy life and to just be still and let God work in my life. Then the fiasco in London happened, and I just could not understand. Like so many other things that have happened in my life, this was another one to add to my list. I was angry and disappointed – not so much for me, but for Michael. I wanted to give him something that would impact him in such a way that he would want to make a difference in other people's lives. I remember sitting in that room in the London airport and worrying so much about Michael. He was alone, confused, and just had no idea what was going on. Late that night, when they finally let him come in the room with me, a huge weight was lifted for both of us. I told him how sorry I was that this had happened, and that if he still wanted to go, I would try to talk to the customs officer to allow him access. It was then that he said, "Mike, if you are not going to be there, I don't want to go. That was half of the fun." It was then that I realized that Michael did not need me to take him across the world to be an impact. He just needed a dad in his life to love him, and I had become that dad for him. In my eyes, I was just his stepdad. In his eyes, I was so much more than that. Now I know how Dad feels about us kids. I never thought that Dad loved the rest of the kids like he did Eric. We knew he loved us, but we also knew Eric was his only biological son, so it was a different kind of love. I no longer feel that way. I look at Michael Costello like I look at Mike Jr. I love Costello like he is my biological son. I did not think that was possible, but it is. And to know that my stepdad (I can hardly even say that word about dad) feels the same about me is indescribable.

I remember being a teenager and could not wait to grow up, get married, and start a family of my own. I so badly wanted to have children and be the dad that I never had (during my young childhood days). I look back over these past 20 years that I have been both a dad and stepdad and think things did not turn out like I thought they would. I recently watched the home video of Maci at one of her gymnastic meets after Rhonda and I divorced. It was the first video I have watched since the car accident nine years ago. Although she started gymnastics while we were still married, I never had a chance to see her perform, as I was either deployed in the military, or just "too busy" working long hours. As I sat there and watched the video, I cried uncontrollably. I longed to go back and be able to be a bigger part of her life. I beat myself up for days afterwards for being a "terrible dad." I know how she and Mike Jr. struggled with our divorce. I carry that guilt with me every day.

Joe gave me an assignment a few weeks ago. He said he wanted me to find five passages in the Bible that spoke to forgiveness. Then he wanted my thoughts on the passage when Jesus was dying on the cross and said, "Father forgive them for they know not what they do." The past couple of weeks, I have really been working on forgiveness. Part of that is forgiving others, and the bigger part is forgiving myself. I remember the first and only time that I confessed to our priest. He said something at the end that I will never forget. He said, "Mike, God has already forgiven you. The most difficult thing will be you forgiving yourself." Wow, did he nail that. When I am speaking, I tell people to stop focusing on the past because we cannot change it. We can't forget our past because it has made us who we are today. But we have to stop focusing on the past and put that energy towards our today and tomorrow. But yet, I do not listen to my own advice. My solution in life is to run when I have to deal with things. For once in my life, I am trying to "be still."

Mom, as I look back over the past 20 years, I realize that as parents, no matter how much we love our kids, we are going to make mistakes. If anyone should hold any grudges in their life, it should be Mike Jr. He was old enough to see the mistakes I made, and most of them impacted his life. Yet he forgives me and still loves me. As I look back over my entire life, there are things that happened in my life as a child and adult that just seemed unforgivable. Yet, it is in the past, and I thought I had forgiven. But, until recently, I don't think that was the case. Like me and every other parent in this world, I know you made mistakes that you wish you could go back and do over. When you gave me my birthday card and you had the "daily bread" that you had drawn for me and it spoke to forgiveness, believe me when I say my heart was already working on it. For the first time in my life, I just wanted to forgive everyone. I was just not sure I wanted the peace that comes with forgiveness. After all, it was those deep emotions that drove me to be where I am today – both the good and the bad. But I realize that I want to be forgiven for the mistakes I made in my life as well. Who am I to be forgiven if I cannot forgive? So, I am writing this long letter to tell you that I forgive you for the choices you made that impacted my life. I don't want you to spend another day thinking that I have not forgiven you and that I do not love you. Now when you pray, ask God to help you forgive yourself. That is far more difficult than forgiving others.

Mom, I have wanted to write a book about my life. I believe it will help with the emotional scars. I don't want to write it from the perspective "look how bad my life was," but more from the perspective that no matter what happens in our lives, we can dictate the outcome. It's not about the speed bumps we encounter or the valleys we walk through, but more about how we handle those things in our life. Mom, your life is as much of a testimony as mine. To get a true depiction of my life, I need to know more. When people read this book and look at the outcome today, it will be an inspiration. Hopefully it will help others learn to forgive themselves and learn to live a more peaceful life. I remember your testimony in Richmond about your life and learning things that night about my life. You could hear a pin drop throughout the entire testimony. I want to have that same impact with this book. But, I can't do it alone. I am asking for your help. I don't want to interview you. I would rather have you write it down. I have found that writing is extremely therapeutic. Also, you can write through the tears as you share your true emotions. If you don't think you can do it, I understand. One of the hardest things I have ever done was write "Maci's Place," but the lives that have been changed are far more rewarding than the pain I experienced as I relived that horrific time. I am going to write as much as I can from memory and pieces that I have learned throughout my life. I am hoping to use your portion to fill in the blanks. Mom, this is something that I have to do for myself. This is me "being still."

Mom, I forgive you. I love you!

A few minutes later, I received the following email from mom:

Hello Son,

I just read the "note" and I can barely see to respond. I am thankful that you are learning the power that is in forgiveness. Jesus said that if you forgive not from your heart, neither will your heavenly father forgive you. I learned the lesson of forgiveness just before I met Clyde. I will share it with you if you would like to hear about it.

I love you, Mike. I have NEVER not loved you and Jim. Through all the stupid mistakes, I truly was trying to find someone to love the three of us and make a happy home. I'm not much good at writing, but I will do my best to get it all down on paper (computer). There is just SOOOOOO much, and the detail really does matter.

I don't know if you remember this or not, but I called you early one morning when I lived in Minnesota (I think). We've lived so many places I'm not really sure. But you lived at Ft. Huachuca. I had been in prayer and felt such an urgency to call all my children and apologize for the failures and heartaches I felt I had caused. They were never intentional. I just didn't know how to be a good parent. Anyway, I woke you up. At the time, I didn't realize the time zone difference. I was so overwhelmed with the grief and urgency that had come upon me. You were the first one I called to ask for forgiveness. I was crying, and you were alarmed and wanted to know if everything was ok. I asked you to forgive me for all the pain I had caused in your life, and you just basically said there was nothing to forgive. We didn't talk very long (I think it was about 6 a.m. your time). When we hung up, I knew that nothing had changed for you, and I didn't expect it to immediately. However, I had done what God laid on my heart, and I have been waiting patiently for the "fullness of time" to come our way. I look forward to our new life as mom and son.

How far back do you want me to go with the story?

I love you so very much......Mom

Mom was right. I did not remember that call. However, the answer she said I gave sounded like something I would have said. All this time, I was harboring unhealthy feelings because I thought my mom never cared about my forgiveness. A few days after sending this email, Mom came to visit me. She told me after much thought and prayer, she did not want to help write the book. She did, however, give me a few details which have been incorporated in the various stories.

At first, I was somewhat angry. But then I had an epiphany. There were parts of my life that I was not going to put in the book because I was ashamed of some of the decisions I made. How hypocritical it was of me to ask my mom to do the same. Little did I realize at the time that God was working on my heart. As I began to look back over my life, I realized that it was better to bring out the positive rather than the negative. We all make mistakes, but it is not the mistake that is important, but the lesson we learn from that mistake.

My heart has changed and continues to change. When I look back over my life, I am no longer angered by what I remember. I am able to see more good than bad. When I speak of this transformation that is happening in my life, I rarely do it with dry eyes. Joe, my mentor and friend, inspired me to just let those negative things go. However, I had to make the decision to actually do it. Joe inspired me. I had to motivate myself.

It seems like my heart is changing on a daily basis. It has not been easy. As a matter of fact, it has been a daily struggle. I felt as if I was giving up my identity. The survivor and fighter in me was becoming more of a soft-hearted and compassionate man. Would that make me weak? I really don't know. Ask me in a year or two, and I will let you know for sure. All I do know is that the battle has been worth it so far. Although I have a long way to go, I do feel peace that I have never felt before.

Introduction

This is the true joy in life – being used for a purpose recognized by yourself as a mighty one; being thoroughly worn out before you are thrown on the scrap heap; being a force of nature instead of a feverish selfish little clod of ailments and grievances complaining that the world will not devote itself to making you happy. ~George Bernard Shaw

I am 36,000 feet above the ground and travelling at Mach .85 – 85% of the speed of sound. In human terms, that is about 500 miles per hour. (Speed in terms of Mach sounds so much more interesting.) My thoughts (as others sleep) are interrupted by the sound of the pilot's voice making what he apparently thought was an important announcement. "Ladies and gentlemen, this is your pilot speaking. For those who may be interested, we are currently passing over Dallas, TX. We are scheduled for an on-time arrival. The weather in Phoenix is…." And that is when he started to lose me. I reached up to adjust my air vent, twisted my body in my seat to pop my back, and then focused on the task at hand.

For the first time since I can remember, the flight was not full. There was an empty seat between myself and the other passenger in row 18. As I began to type once again, my peripheral vision caught the glance of my row buddy in the direction of my laptop. He was probably wondering what I was writing that required me to type so ferociously. You see, I am not one of those guys who can type and look at the monitor. I only use two fingers on each of my hands, but I have been told that I am the fastest four-finger typist many have ever seen. It may have appeared that I was mad at my keyboard, but I had so much to say, and my fingers, quite simply, just could not keep up with my mind.

Now I have stopped typing altogether and started collecting my thoughts. I began the three-finger dance (index, middle, and ring finger lightly bouncing in succession) next to the mouse on my laptop. If I had long fingernails, my finger dancing would have become very disruptive to those around me in a very short matter of time. I know, because if some-one sitting near me was doing the finger dance or clicking on their pen continuously as they were deep in thought, or tapping their notebook with their pencil as they listened to their music, I know what I would want to do. I would want to locate one of the nearest exits (that were so graciously pointed out in the pre-flight safety demonstration), move at a rapid pace to the exit that provided the least resistance, and remove myself from the moving projectile travelling at Mach .85! Obviously, I am just kidding about exiting the aircraft. The last thing I would ever want is to be seated next to a passenger that just so happened to have read this book and taken that last thought seriously. I think the scene would go something like this.

I am seated in the window seat, buckled in with my Blackberry clipped on the seat in front of me. A passenger finds her seat next to me. We say hello and have a 30 second casual conversation before she gets this look in her eyes. She proceeds to ask, "Are you the guy who wrote Strong

Finish?" Of the 121 copies sold, this lady just happened to be one who had purchased the book. My first thought is flattery. My superego kicks in for a nanosecond. Her very next movement is quick and seemed well rehearsed. She taps the call button. I use the word "tap" loosely. For a second, I thought the button would surely shatter into 17 pieces of plastic designed by the lowest bidder. She then asks to be seated anywhere away from me.

So, that is why I want to make it perfectly clear that I was kidding about removing myself from the plane. Even though I love visiting Dallas, I certainly do not want that to be my resting place. At this point, I am kind of chuckling to myself. Had my passenger friend sitting in the aisle seat been awake, he may have thought I was a little nuts. However, when you travel as much as I do, you have to find some form of entertainment. The look on the faces of 131 passengers as I struggled to open the emergency exit seemed quite comical at the time. Now, I really must reiterate that I am only kidding and would NEVER consider actually acting this out.

My self-humoring moment is over, and I am back deep in thought. As the three-finger dance continues, the words "strong finish" run through my mind. Many authors and speakers long before me have provided motivational stories about what it means to finish strong. I am certainly not the first to write about it, and I will most certainly not be the last. In his book titled "Finish Strong" to teen athletes, Dan Green said it best, "It's more than a statement, it's an attitude." I agree whole heartedly with Dan. However, I want to take it a step further. What does "strong finish" actually mean to me? How have I applied it in my life? What lessons have I learned? More importantly, is my "strong finish" making a difference in other people's lives?

What words can I possibly put on paper that will make an impact on you?

Then the answer came to me. I could write about celebrities, professional athletes, politicians, war heroes, and other infamous people who have overcome adversity. I could write about Albert Einstein, who could not speak fluently until he was nine, how he was expelled from school on numerous occasions, and had the Nobel Prize taken from him by the Germans because he was Jewish. Helen Keller, who, at the age of two, was stuck with an illness that left her deaf and blind, but was considered "America's First Lady of Courage." Walt Disney was fired from a Kansas City newspaper because he was not considered creative enough. Alexander Graham Bell suffered from dyslexia, resulting in poor grades in school. Of course, he went on to invent the telephone. Like Bell, Thomas Edison suffered from dyslexia. He had great difficulty with speaking and was considered too dumb to be in school. He was holding the other students back. Not only did he invent the light bulb, but he went on to patent over 1000 other inventions.

There are more. George Patton was one of the greatest generals to ever serve our country. Throughout his entire life, he could barely read and had to memorize all of his lectures. Abraham Lincoln, 16th President of the United States, is one of the most revered figures in American history. His challenge started at a young age when his mother died and his father felt school was a waste of time. He taught himself to be a lawyer, became a senator, and then the President. While in office, Lincoln lost his 12-year-old son to typhoid fever. Julio Igelsias was turned down by the school choir and was told he could not carry a tune. After attending the American Academy of Dramatic Arts, Lucille

Ball's mother received a letter stating "to stop spending her money because her daughter would never make it."

The list goes on and on, and book after book has been written about these and many others with one goal in mind – inspire the reader. So, why write another book about famous people who have overcome adversity to achieve great success? After all, who am I that I could possibly fathom their true feelings and emotions as they battled through their challenges? I could conduct my own research and try to imagine what these well-known icons went through. I could hold my breath and wait for a request for an interview from those who are still alive. Even if I pursued both of these options and was successful, would it still go down as just another motivational book? Most likely. So, in the words of the great Frank Sinatra, "I did it my way."

As you begin to read "Strong Finish," you will not turn too many pages before you start noticing a pattern. Every story is either based on my own personal experiences, someone who is currently in my life, or someone who has crossed my path along my journey. Some of these stories will be about overcoming adversity. Some will display acts of heroism. Others will portray random acts of kindness and how the smallest gestures can make the largest impact. The common thread that is woven throughout this book is that of true raw emotion. The guesswork has been removed. This book is not just for those who are currently faced with adversity and challenges and looking for answers to overcome and excel. This book is also for those who are "smooth sailing" and are looking for ways to make a difference – to make their mark upon this earth. Regardless of where you are on your own personal journey, this book will accomplish one thing – Inspiration. Why would it inspire but not motivate? Inspiration gets you started. Motivation will keep you going.

This book will serve as the spark or the igniter. The motivational part is your choice.

Some of the people in this book are nameless. And that's what makes their story so powerful. These nameless people made such a huge impact in my life, that I now look for ways to become nameless as well. Sounds confusing, right? As you read, you will begin to understand.

The "fasten seatbelt" sign is about to be illuminated as we start making our final approach into Phoenix. I am finally almost home. Before powering down my laptop, I would like to offer my personal "pre-flight safety demonstration" as you begin this journey:

> I welcome all passengers aboard this journey to wherever your final destination may be. Please listen carefully to these safety instructions – even if you are a frequent traveller – as they are specific to this journey.

> All of your luggage should be safely stowed in the overhead compartments or under the seat in front of you. If you "forget about your luggage" along the journey, that is perfectly fine and actually expected. In preparing for takeoff, make sure your mind is cleared and distractions are locked away. Click your seatbelt closed and make sure it fits snugly across your hips. This could be a bumpy ride, so please keep the seatbelts fastened at all times.

> I would like to point out the exits. There are only two exits on this journey – they are the front and back covers of this book. Please take a moment to

identify those exits. There are not any strip lights to guide you to the exit. If you need to exit, place your left hand on the front cover and your right hand on the back cover, and simply bring them together.

This book will also serve as your life preserver in the event of an emergency. If you should need the life preserver, it will be your choice on whether you use it or not. There are not instructions on how to use the life preserver, because there is no wrong way to use it.

If at this time, you feel the need to end this journey before it begins, feel free to exercise your right to exit at this time. For the remainder of you who are on your life-changing journey of inspiration and motivation, we are about to take off. Sit back and enjoy your trip.

Chapter 1

Strong Finish – What does it mean?

Guiding Principle: "Today is the first day of the rest of your life. Make a difference now." ~Michael S. Miller

> *How wonderful it is that nobody need wait a single moment before starting to improve the world.*
> ~Anne Frank

One of the first times I recall using the words "strong finish" in my daily life started back in 1998 with my daughter, Maci. She was four years old at the time, and my wife decided to put her in gymnastics. Maci learned one of the most important lessons of gymnastics at her first lesson. No matter how successful or terribly wrong you think your performance went, you always need to have a "strong finish" after each routine. The "strong finish" required two basic steps – the stuck landing and the actual finish. When the gymnast lands a tumbling pass, vault, or dismount without moving his/her feet, it is called a stuck landing. The aim of every gymnast is to stick the landing. If the gymnast moves his/her feet at all, it is a deduction. The goal is to appear as if you have ultimate control and know exactly when your feet will hit the ground. The "stick" can be the difference between a good routine and an extraordinary routine. It can mean the difference between winning the gold medal and not medaling at all.

Once the gymnast sticks the landing, the last move they make is the real "strong finish" – feet together, back slightly arched, and arms extended above the head. It is one of the most graceful movements in all of sports. This is the gymnast's signature on their routine. This is their way of saying, "I did my best. I have had performances that were much better, and some that were worse. But today, at this very moment in time, I gave my best." This is their statement to the world.

Upon returning home from the first lesson, our instructions from the coach were to have Maci practice her "strong finish." No matter where we were or what we were doing, when Maci heard us say "strong finish," she had to throw her arms up in the air. It did not take very long before it became an automatic response for Maci. I remember one particular time when we were at the store, and Maci was walking in front of us with her little friend. They were walking through the toy aisle and just chatting away about the different dolls and outfits that would look so cute on their dolls. I thought this would be a good time for a test, so I said, "Maci, strong finish." Without even thinking or even the slightest pause in her conversation, she threw up her arms over her head. It was the cutest thing, and from that point forward, we often got a kick out of having Maci conduct her "strong finish" in the most peculiar places.

That was my first real introduction to a "strong finish." Then as my boys grew older, and the level of competition increased in their respective sports, the phrase "strong finish," or "finish strong," became routine. Like the words imply, they always came near the final minutes of the game. You could hear the coach yell, "Two minutes left. Let's finish strong." I, myself, am guilty as well of offering words of encouragement for the "strong finish." My son, Michael, has been playing soccer since he was four. At the time I am writing this book, he is almost seventeen years old and is a very talented player. I love going to soccer matches because it is one of the few sports where you are right there on the sidelines and sometimes mere feet from the players. As they run pass the sidelines, you can see the sweat and hear their heavy breathing. Michael normally plays the entire game (90 minutes) with only a short break during each 45 minute half. Near the end of the game, if by chance the play happens to be in close proximity to where we are sitting on the sidelines, I always try to encourage him. I have my stopwatch going, and I know exactly how much time is left in the game. Whether we are winning or losing, he can expect to hear these words from me, "Michael, only two and a half minutes left. Leave it all on the field. Strong finish." I know he is whipped. He has played the majority of the game. He has been running constantly. He has been kicked, elbowed, knocked down, stepped on, and every muscle in his body is in agony. Just like most champions, even though he feels like quitting, that adrenaline seems to kick in, and he gives everything he has to give until that final whistle blows. He finishes strong.

Let's talk football – specifically professional football. I have witnessed some of the best football ever played in the last two minutes of a game. Now granted, if it is a blowout and the winning team has the ball when the play resumes after the two minute warning, the game is quite boring. The team gets in their "victory formation" and the quarterback takes a knee and lets the clock wind down. It is a much different story if a team is down by a touchdown or field goal, and they have the ball after the two minute warning. Add on the fact that they don't have any timeouts, and it is some of the best football ever played. You see a hurry-up offense where there is no huddle and the quarterback is calling the play at the line of scrimmage. You witness some of the most spectacular passes and catches by these superstars. The plays that are called are completely different than what you would see in the first 58 minutes of the game. The risk factor is elevated exponentially. Regardless of the results, when the time runs out, you can bet it will probably be one of the best games of the week.

I have often sat on the couch after watching the losing team battle it out in the final two minutes and fail to get the ball in the end zone for the game winning score, and try to analyze what they could have done better. There have been many times when I wish the head coach would pick up the phone and invite me to come in and watch the game film and give my feedback. I am one of a million guys who often feel like we can outcoach that head coach any day of the week and twice on Sunday. Then we eventually snap out of our fantasy world and back to reality. But here is my thought. Why not play the entire game like it is the last two minutes, and you are coming from behind to try to get that game-winning score? Ok, I know that is not a reality. If you really sit down and think about what is entailed and the physical and mental energy that is expended in that two minute rush, it is probably humanly impossible (at least from a physical aspect). However, your attitude and how you approach the game is what makes the difference.

No matter what we do, our attitude is our driving force in life. Countries lose wars often times because they "lose their will to fight." In other words, their attitude went from "I can" to "I can't." Lou Holtz says, "Ability is what you are capable of doing. Motivation determines what you do. Attitude determines how well you do it."

Countless books have been written about having the "right attitude." I just went to Amazon.com and typed in "attitude," and a list of 39,186 books were displayed within seconds. Over the years, I have read many books about attitude, and all of the authors were in agreement: *your attitude determines your altitude*!

Author Tom Clancy had a dream when he was working at his insurance agency in Maryland. His dream was to someday write a book that would entertain "millions" of people. He was quoted in an issue of *Nation's Business* magazine as saying, "There are two kinds of people in the world. There are people who go for the dream and either succeed or fail. Even if they fail, they succeed, because at least they tried. But if you're the other kind of person, afraid to go for the dream, then about the time you retire, you'll have the condo down in Florida, and you'll be down there in the elephant graveyard waiting to die, and you'll think, gosh, what if when I was 30 I had gone ahead and sailed around the world or bought that airplane I always wanted to buy?"

He went on to write his first of many best-selling books, *The Hunt for Red October*, which was published in October of 1984. At a business luncheon a few years later, he told the audience, "Nothing is as real as a dream. And if you go for it, something really good is going to happen to you. You may grow old, but you'll never really get old. Because if you hold on to the dream you had when you were in high school and college, you have a fighting chance to stay the person you were. Just keep chasing after the rainbows, and you'll stay young forever."

Tom Clancy had the right attitude. And look at the "altitude" that his "attitude" has taken him!

If you watch ESPN on a regular basis, you will see professional athletes who have a "strong finish" all the time. We also hear about people who are nearing the end of their life journey and decide to do something that will be their legacy. I have known people who were terminally ill and made as much of an impact (if not more) during their last days than they did their entire life.

I think I know the reason why. Most of us have good intentions, but we are huge procrastinators. We say we are going to make changes tomorrow, or next week, or next year. Then, whether it is age or an illness, we realize that we do not have as many tomorrows as we have yesterdays. It is our two minute warning in life, and we begin our hurry-up offense so we can make an impact and leave our mark on this earth.

Remember this important fact: "Someday" is not a day of the week. Monday, Tuesday, Wednesday, Thursday, Friday, Saturday, and Sunday are days of the week. And while I recognize that for most people it's hard not to say "someday" I'll get started, just remember that "someday" is not an option! Pick another day and make it happen. As the famous Nike commercial told us a few years ago: "Just do it!"

When I look back over my life, I think about all the missed opportunities of making a difference in people's lives. I am 40 years old as I write this book, and if I am lucky, I still have half of my life left. It has been that kind of attitude though that accounts for those missed opportunities. With that kind of thinking, I will probably wait until I am 65 or 70 years old, and life slows down a bit. Then I can focus on others and figure out what my legacy will be. I will still have a good 10-15 years to dedicate my life to doing something good – to leave my mark. That's not bad. We all know people who have done much less and are still good people, right? With those kinds of numbers, I am sure to get the eulogy of a hero. At this point, I hope you are thinking what I am thinking. What a jerk. Does he really believe the crap he is writing? Somebody needs to give him a wakeup call.

The good news is that I did get that wakeup call. The bad news is that I got the wakeup call. I know. I am not making sense again. It does not have to make sense right now. It will become clear enough as you continue to read. The point to all of this is that I do not want to wait until I am near the end of what I think my life is going to be and then start working on my "strong finish." The most valuable lesson that I have learned (as well as a few others mentioned in the book) in my life is that none of us is promised tomorrow. We know this. We have heard it our entire lives. It is the basis of many of our values. But knowing it and actually believing it are two entirely different things. Most of the people I know, or people who have crossed my path, believe that their tomorrow will come. Most of them believe they are going to live a long life and have plenty of time left for their "strong finish." I am not here to judge or criticize any of them. That is our human nature. It is part of our genetic makeup.

I do hope that this book will serve as a wakeup call for each and every one of you. I do not want you to get the same wakeup call that I and some of the others got. It really does not have to be that difficult. I am a realist though. I know this book will not be a decision tree moment in most of your lives. I am sure that it will inspire many, but I believe that few will be motivated. Remember, it is my job to ignite or inspire. It is your choice to be motivated.

I always thought that if I had been placed in certain positions of authority in my life, then I could make some serious impactful changes. When I first found out that I had been selected to attend Officer Candidate School, I thought that I would be able to change the Army as a young Second Lieutenant. It did not take me long to see the error in my judgment. Although I had good intentions, I realized I could only impact those who were in my command. To take it a step further, I could only impact those in my command who were open to being impacted. The number that I initially thought I could make an impact on and the actual number was exponentially smaller. That was ok though. As the years passed, I realized that those small numbers start adding up. Then a few years ago, Joe, my close friend and mentor, told me something that brought it all into perspective. "If you change a life, you change a generation." That is POWER-FUL!

As you read this book, here are the two points that I want you to think about when you are planning your "strong finish":

1. Don't wait until tomorrow to start your "strong finish."
2. You don't have to impact the world. Just focus on changing one life at a time.

I am not perfect. I am actually far from it. I have made mistakes in my past. I will make mistakes today. I will make mistakes tomorrow. I don't have it all figured out. What I do know is that you have the opportunity to learn from my experiences and the experiences of those in this book. As my dear friend, Steve Falcon, once told me, "Mike, you have the opportunity to change many lives." Although Steve has since passed, I can still hear those words of encouragement like it was yesterday. I now offer those same words of encouragement to you.

When speaking to an audience, I often finish my speech with a story about making a difference. Instead of concluding the book with the story, I wanted to introduce it in the beginning so it will be just a memory away. It's called The Starfish Story, and it was written by Loren Eiseley.

The Starfish Story

Once upon a time, there was a wise man who used to go to the ocean to do his writing. He had a habit of walking on the beach before he began his work. One day, as he was walking along the shore, he looked down the beach and saw a human figure moving like a dancer. He smiled to himself at the thought of someone who would dance to the day, and so, he walked faster to catch up. As he got closer, he noticed that the figure was that of a young man, and that what he was doing was not dancing at all. The young man was reaching down to the shore, picking up small objects, and throwing them into the ocean.

He came closer still and called out, "Good morning! May I ask what it is that you are doing?"

The young man paused, looked up, and replied, "Throwing starfish into the ocean."

"I must ask, then, why are you throwing starfish into the ocean?" asked the somewhat startled wise man.

To this, the young man replied, "The sun is up and the tide is going out. If I don't throw them in, they'll die."

Upon hearing this, the wise man commented, "But, young man, do you not realize that there are miles and miles of beach, and there are starfish all along every mile? You can't possibly make a difference!"

At this, the young man bent down, picked up yet another starfish, and threw it into the ocean. As it met the water, he said, "I made a difference on that one!"

Do not wait another day to begin your "strong finish." Every day presents itself with opportunities for a "strong finish." You made a difference in someone's life yesterday. You will make a difference in someone's life today. Tomorrow you will make a difference again. The question is whether it will be a positive difference or negative difference. That is your choice and in your full control. A smile, a friendly gesture, a nice word to a neighbor or co-worker, a hand-written note to your spouse, or a simple word of encouragement to your child as they leave for school could make a huge positive difference in their life. Choose wisely and finish strong.

Chapter 2

Is Your Cross too Heavy to Bear?

Guiding Principle: Things may appear dismal at best. You may feel like no one has ever suffered like you are now. Look around you though. Someone will have it worse than you. Healing comes in taking the focus off of you and placing it on someone else.

Dare to reach out your hand into the darkness, to pull another hand into the light. ~Norman B. Rice

The young man was at the end of his rope. Seeing no way out, he dropped to his knees in prayer. "Lord, I can't go on," he said. "I have too heavy a cross to bear."

The Lord replied, "My son, if you can't bear its weight, just place your cross inside this room. Then, pick out any cross you wish."

The man was filled with relief. "Thank you, Lord," he sighed, and he did as he was told. Walking through the room, he saw many crosses, some so large the tops were not even visible. Then, he spotted a tiny cross leaning against a far wall. "I'd like that one, Lord," he whispered.

And the Lord replied, "My son, that is the cross you just brought in."

I look back on my life and the things I went through and realize I am a better person because of it. But, if I had to go back and do it over again, I still would not do it. There were just things in my life that if given the choice, I would not have done. Although I feel like I am a better person, I still do not understand why God chose this particular path for me. I echo the words of Mother Theresa: "God, I know you said you would not put on us more than we can bear. I just wish you did not believe in me so much." Of all the things in my life that I have had to overcome, there is one event that shook and crumbled the very foundation of my world. For those who have heard me speak or have read my book, Maci's Place, you know the event I am referring to. Please bear with me as I share the most defining event in my life with the others.

It was a little after 7 P.M. May 11, 2001, when I got the call. My son had been involved in a car accident. I was being told by the attending physician that Maci had a 20% chance of surviving, and Michael had about a 50% chance of surviving. I could not believe what I was hearing. This is the call you always hear about, but never get yourself. Michael pulled through surgery, and as the night passed, he progressively got better. Maci's case was just the opposite. The following morning, Maci went to be with God.

I managed to hold myself together for 11 more days while my son recovered in the hospital. I was in a state of shock, and many details of those 11 days are still a blur to me. The memories that are still very clear are:

- Seeing a life support machine for the first time in my life, and it connected to my daughter.
- Seeing my son with tubes down his throat and open wounds on his body.
- Walking the path between my son's bed and my daughter's bed the very first night.
- Watching both of my children fight for their lives.
- Holding Maci's hands as she went to be with God.
- Attending the funeral.
- Attending the memorial services with Michael at their school.
- The day Michael came home from the hospital.

I believe most people handle a horrific event such as this much better than I did. People used to tell me how strong I was, and I hated hearing that. First of all, they had no idea how I was trying to cope. Second, what other choice did I have? I had to learn to live with the loss. Learning to live with the loss of a child is not a destination. It is a life-long journey. I made my journey so much more difficult than it had to be. Instead of turning to God, I turned my back on Him and ran as far as I could. I did not want to have anything to do with God, who (at the time) I thought took my daughter from this world.

There are some things that transpired in my life over those next two years that I am ashamed to mention. I turned to illegal drugs, prescription drugs, and alcohol, and made some very poor choices in the name of grief. I pushed everything and everyone who cared about me out of my world. I thought if I could distance myself from the things and people I care about, then the pain would be less intense if I lost them. People say they had to hit rock bottom before they could begin to recover. Well, I did a nose dive through my "rock bottom" and just kept on going. All of these things were short lived and provided a temporary numbness to my pain.

Make no mistake about it. I will offer no excuses. I am responsible for those choices and live with them every day of my life. However, I have to look ahead. I have found that there is healing in writing and helping others who are in similar situations. Throughout this journey, I have also met people whose cross is so much larger than mine. I am reminded of the quote that says, "I used to complain about having no shoes until I saw a man with no feet." I have met people along my journey who have lost their only child. I have met others who have lost all of their children and a spouse. I have even met some who have lost a child and a parent in the same accident. So yes, I have gone through a traumatic event and have earned the right to grieve, but I have no right to ask God for a lighter cross to bear. As soon as I pulled myself away from my self-thrown pity party, I realized that the cross I was bearing was not impossible.

The key to surviving any event in our lives is allowing others to help us. Even when Jesus was forced to carry His cross, He too stumbled and needed help. And guess what, He let Himself be helped. He did not say to Himself and others, "I am God. I need help from no man." On the contrary, He led by example. If Jesus can accept assistance with His cross, who are we not to do the same?

I would not say that the journey gets easier with time, but the pain does get less intense. I continue to learn to live with the loss of Maci, but I have learned to be happy again. I can't put a finger on the day when I started smiling again. It just kind of happened. Having my son, Mike Jr., in my life has been the main contributing factor to my new life. My friends are different, I am remarried, and I live around most of my family. I still struggle daily. You read the foreword that Joe wrote, and I am still battling with my demons. Just last week, a group of dads in our neighborhood Bible study group were talking about the Father-Daughter Valentines Dance. I was surprised by the amount of pain I felt, even after almost 10 years since Maci has passed. In a few days from the time I am writing this chapter, she would have celebrated her 17th birthday. I won't see her graduate high school and college. I won't get to walk her down the aisle and give her away. There are many things I will not get to do with Maci in this life. However, I have made the choice to move forward. It won't happen overnight, but it will happen. Along the way, if you see me stumble with my cross, feel free to help. If I see your cross is too much to bear at times, you can count on me to relieve you of that burden – even if for just a short time.

Our Dance

She runs into the kitchen
Looks at the invitation on the refrigerator door.
Today is the Father – Daughter Dance
The night she has been waiting for.

She wonders if he knows
This is her favorite night of the year.
Tonight it's just she and her daddy
It is a day she holds so dear.

He walks into the kitchen
His coffee in his hand.
Tonight he gets to dance with his daughter
A special treat for any man.

He wonders if she still loves this night
Like she did way back when.
He wonders if she knows he wishes
This night would never end.

She went and bought a brand new dress
A pair of shoes was also on her list.
Mommy will fix her hair real nice
And place a flower on her wrist.

He'll take that suit out of his closet
It's not new but barely worn.
He only wears it on special occasions
Like the night when she was born.

She'll walk onto the dance floor
Her daddy following close behind.
She'll try to dance as well as mommy
By not stepping on his toes this time.

He follows her onto the dance floor
She's not that tiny little girl she used to be.
Oh how he wishes he could go back to the time
When she used to dance upon his feet.

She moves with her daddy to the music
He's a good dancer but that's no surprise.
She wonders if he knows
He'll always be a hero in her eyes.

These are the moments he lives for
He knows too soon they will be gone.
But the night he danced with his daughter
Will be a memory that will forever live on.

Tonight is their special night
They both know it without saying a word.
Tonight exists just the two of them
Dancing in each other's world.

Dedicated to every dad who has ever danced with his little girl.

Mike Miller
January 31, 2011
In memory of my little girl. I will always remember our dance.
"Hugs and Kisses"

Chapter 3

Looking Through the Rearview Mirror

Guiding Principle: Occasionally glance into life's rearview mirror as a reminder of lessons learned. Spend the majority of your time looking ahead.

> *I expect to pass through life but once. If, therefore, there be any kindness I can show, or any good thing I can do to any fellow being, let me do it now, and not defer or neglect it, as I shall not pass this way again.*
> ~William Penn

As I previously mentioned in the Introduction (and for those who skipped the introduction), my goal is not to tell the same stories about famous individuals who looked straight in the eyes of adversity, wrestled it to the ground, and became successful as a result. Sure, there would be some entertaining stories. But if you are still reading, it means you are looking for more than just entertainment. What can I as an ordinary human being do to become extraordinary? That is the question for everyone who is reading this book. The answer is in the personal stories that I will share with you. However, before getting into the stories, it is necessary to understand a little more about my life and some of the challenges and adversity I have faced.

Before going any further, I want to make something perfectly clear. I am not writing this book out of self-pity or to honor myself. I am not looking for sympathy or accolades. If this is the end result, then I have failed. My goal is to inspire you so much that you will choose to be motivated.

I attended a National Speaker's Association Conference a few years ago with several hundred other professional speakers. I decided to sit in one of the workshops for what I thought would be designed for the current motivational speaker. I was surprised to find many speakers who spoke on other topics, but were interested in being a motivational speaker. I was somewhat humored by a certain gentleman's question: "I have had a pretty good life. I really have not had anything bad happen to me, and I certainly have not had to overcome any more adversity than the average person. That being the case, how do I become a motivational speaker?" No one, including the workshop leader, could really give this guy a good answer. I had my own opinion, but kept it to myself. If he is reading this book, he now has my answer to his question. "Unless you have had a crappy life and had to overcome challenges and adversity that is well beyond the norm, it is impossible to be a genuine motivational speaker."

If there are any motivational speakers who are reading this book and disagree with my answer, you probably fall into that category and are about to exercise your right to exit this journey. That is your choice, and should you make that choice, just know something before you leave. It is my answer and my opinion. It is my belief, and this is why. As a speaker, I must make an emotional connection with my audience. Some can do that because you can tell a great story. Others (like me) have a great story to tell. It is a story based on personal experiences. Although the audience may not have experienced the same exact experiences, we have experiences in which we share the same exact emotions. And thus, the bond between speaker and audience is formed. There is a difference in knowledge and actual experience. Would you seek parental advice from someone who has never had children? How about marital advice from someone who has never been married? Ok, enough said.

Now, back to those who are still with me. I am not much of an artist, but I would like to paint you a picture that will give you a small glimpse into my life. Since I can't speak to you in person, it is my hope that this picture will be the emotional connection between my words and you. Each stroke of the brush will reveal a new experience in my life. Like you, as we experience bad things in our life, it is never a pleasurable trip as we are going through it. As we gaze through the windshield of life, we wonder how long this particular leg of our journey will last. There are no signs that give us the mileage to the next rest stop. We wonder why it's happening to us and no one else. We question what we did in the past to deserve this trial. Sometimes, we even doubt the existence of God or simply choose not to allow him in our lives. That last one is a tough one, and one I can speak to from my personal experiences.

Eventually, we do finally get through the experience and can view it from our rearview mirror. Now we have a choice to make. We are no longer in survival mode and can think more logically. We can simply attempt to put it out of our minds forever, or we can learn from the experience. It's not about the challenges or adversities (speed bumps) that we encounter along life's highway that matters. What is the most important thing is how we react to those speed bumps. That is what defines who we are and who we are to become. I have to be honest. Most of my life, as I looked through my rearview mirror, I made the wrong choice. I can't go back and change that though. All I can do is look forward and try to make the right choice in the future. That's my "strong finish."

Chapter 4

When Life Throws You Lemons

**Guiding Principle: Making the choice is the easy part.
Acting on that choice takes courage.**

*I've learned that you shouldn't go through life with a
catcher's mitt on both hands. You need to be able to
throw something back.* ~Maya Angelou

Last year, I delivered a keynote speech titled, "Who
Decides?" The driving point to the entire presentation was
that we all make our own choices in life. Many times we
cannot control the circumstances we are faced with, but we
can control the outcome. We make hundreds of choices a
day – some consciously and some subconsciously.

While attending a Compassionate Friends meeting last year,
there was one particular lady who stood out among everyone
else. We all had something in common, and that was the
reason we were gathered in that room. We had all lost a
child and were looking for answers on how to live this "new
life" without our child. Diane's situation was a little different.

She had lost her son and her mother in a bus accident. She had sustained numerous injuries herself, but none as deep as the emotional injuries she was trying to survive.

You see, when you are going through something in your life, as tragic as it may seem, there is always someone else who is going through an even tougher trial. "I used to complain about having no shoes until I saw a man with no feet." I am reminded of that quote every day. After losing my daughter, I could not imagine anything worse in the world. Then I met Diane, who lost her child and mother. Then I met a couple who lost both of their children. Then, there was Stephanie, who lost her only child and husband when a drunk driver crossed the line on the way home from a Friday night football game. I could write an entire book about people I have met whose losses are unspeakable. Still, we decide how we are going to take those cards and play our hand.

That particular night, Diane spoke up for the first time. She had been coming for several months, but chose to remain silent. Tonight was different. "It has been six months since my son and mother died in the car accident," she started. "I have been struggling with who I should grieve for. When I grieve for my son, I feel guilty that I am not grieving for my mom. When I grieve for my mom, I feel that I should be grieving for my son. The past six months have almost killed me. I know that it is not what my mom or son would want if they were here right now."

It was Diane's next words that made the greatest impact on me. "Tonight, I choose to live. Judge me or not, that is my choice." Diane never attended another meeting after that night. I applaud her courage. Normally it takes years to actually begin living a somewhat normal life – not that there is much of "normal" in anything we do after losing a child. I am sure Diane is still struggling, but she had the courage to make a choice. Many times, making the actual choice is more difficult than actually acting on that choice.

We have all heard the quote, "When life hands you lemons, make lemonade." The idea is that we should make something positive out of a negative. I agree. However, I would like to take it a step further. Many of the trials and tribulations we go through are a result of the choices we have made along our journey. We choose what level of education we will pursue. We choose who we are going to have relationships with. We choose our friends. We choose where we are going to work and the career we are going to have. We make these choices with the best of intentions, but sometimes the results are far from what we expected.

So, what do I mean when I say to take it a step further? Here is my rendition of that quote. "When the world hands you lemons, throw them back!" As I prefaced, we cannot control ALL of our circumstances, but we can control some of them. So, for those things in our life that we can control, don't give anyone else the power to control them for you. That's what it means to throw the lemons back. For those situations that are out of our control, make the best of them with the choices you make. Make lemonade.

It takes courage to make the right choices for the right reasons. The main difference between a leader and a manager is this: Managers do things right. Leaders do the right things. Every successful business needs both managers and leaders. The main ingredient that sets them apart though is courage. Anybody can be a leader, regardless of the position they have in an organization or the number of abbreviations they have after their name. However, you must have courage to do the right things and to make the right decisions.

It takes courage to stand up for what we believe in when we are standing alone. It takes courage to step outside our comfort zone and try something new. It takes courage to admit our weaknesses and failures. It takes even more courage to continue even after we have failed over and over again. It takes courage to walk away from a job because you can no longer ethically and morally do what is being asked. It takes courage to travel the high road and make amends to that friend or family member who wronged you. Courage is a choice – a choice that only you can make. What you decide to choose today will determine who you will be tomorrow. Even deeper than that, the choices you make today could determine someone else's destiny.

At the age of 18, she was kidnapped and taken into the mountains of northern California where she was held captive for several weeks. She had been dating her captor, and after several attempts to break off the relationship, he took matters into his own hands. Throughout this time of captivity, she was forced to participate in drug use activities and was sexually assaulted on numerous occasions. Somehow, her father found out where she was being held and showed up to attempt to rescue her. His life would have been taken had she chosen to go with him. So she made the choice to stay and eventually escaped. Little did she know that this choice would pale in comparison to a choice she would soon be faced with.

She had been raped and forced to do drugs. Shortly after escaping, she learned she was pregnant. Her family and friends told her she should abort the baby. No one would blame her or judge her. After all, that was no way to bring a child into the world. Yet, she made her choice.

At nineteen years old, it was time to head to the hospital to deliver her second child. She had been married with her first child, but was since divorced. She felt the labor pains coming on. Alone and scared, she drove herself to the hospital. No one was there to meet her. She checked herself into the hospital and suffered several hours of labor before finally giving birth to a baby boy. No one was there to hold her hand and offer her support. No one was there to celebrate in her joy. She was alone. Why? Because everyone told her she should abort the child. Yet against everyone's advice, she chose life. Because of that choice, I now have my life. Yes, that courageous woman was my mom.

Mom, I know you are reading this book, so I just want to pause very briefly and say "Thank you." Thank you for choosing life – specifically my life. My personal opinion is that it is one of your finer choices!

If this book changes your life, you can thank me later for having the courage to write it. However, the real person who needs to be thanked is my mom. Yes, she made some bad choices, and life threw her lemons. However, against everyone else's beliefs, I am glad of the choice she made back in 1969. That choice is like a ripple effect. I can only hope that I have the courage to make a choice that makes a difference in a life. After all, I feel that is my responsibility. Responsibility or not, it is still a choice. So I choose to have a "throw back the lemons" party, and you are all invited. The guest of honor? Who else...Mom!

I never knew my biological father and still don't to this day. I have never seen a picture of him, so I can only imagine what he looks like. To be honest, I rarely even give it much thought. When I was 14, my mom married the man who I consider to be my dad. As the saying goes, "Anyone can be a father, but it takes someone special to be a dad." Another great choice made by Mom.

Here is the Reader's Digest version of my childhood. I bounced back and forth between my mom (and the men in her life) and my grandparents for most of my childhood. I attended 15 different schools from K-12. I was exposed to drugs and alcohol at a very young age. I smoked my first joint when I was eight years old. I suffered from verbal and physical abuse throughout my younger years. For the most part, I thought my life was normal. However, the older I got, the more I noticed that my life was anything but the norm. As a young child, the few friends that I can recall having had a completely different life. Although my young mind thought they were just the exception, I still longed to be like them. Many nights, I would cry myself to sleep.

So, there it is in a nutshell. I share this with you because I have seen many people make excuses for their choices and blame it on their upbringing. They use that part of their life as a scapegoat, and for what they consider to be a free pass to make bad choices. It's like they have a charge card that they use to charge their excuses to for the poor decisions they make. Here comes an excuse. Charge it. CHA-CHING! Here comes the ruthless side of me. Stop making excuses for your bad decisions. Quit blaming it on a bad childhood. Grow up, take responsibility, and be accountable. Life is not easy for anyone. So maybe your life was a little more difficult than most. Mine too. Get over it. The world does not care, and neither should you. Learn from it and make the world a better place. Be a better person and give someone the opportunity you did not have. On a softer note, the world does not care, but I do, and so do others who have similar experiences. Become a starfish thrower!

Chapter 5

Life's Defining Moments

**Guiding Principle: If you say you will deliver, you
better be the world's best mailman.**

> *Every action in our lives touches on some chord that will
> vibrate in eternity.* ~Edwin Hubbel Chapin

We all have those moments in our life – moments that
change our lives. I don't believe there are very many of
them though. Some moments are more life-changing than
others, such as the birth of a child, a near death experience,
or simply an experience that prompts a look into our life.
Some of these moments trigger an immediate change, while
others take years. We can look back on our life and pretty
quickly point out those life-defining moments. However, I
believe that we have had some life-changing moments in our
lives that we just have not realized yet. I have had several of
those moments in my life, and I have discussed a few of
them in this book. This story happens to be one of those life-
defining moments that waited several years, until I became a
father, before it presented itself.

"They want your bike!" Those are the words that were coming out of my brother's mouth as he came running down the street. With tears pouring from his eyes and out of breath, he said it again. "They *<deep breath and tears>* want *<deep breath and tears>* your *<deep breath and tears>* bike."

Before moving forward, let's rewind a little. It was one of those few Christmases that I actually remember getting actual gifts. We were living with my mom and her boyfriend. I don't remember much about that guy, but I believe he was one of the decent guys in my mom's life. I am guessing I was about five years old, so that would make my brother, Jimmy (what I called him), almost seven years old. He opened his gift and was elated! Jimmy had his very own stereo with an 8-track cassette tape of John Denver. If that was his gift, I could only imagine what I was getting. I knew it had to be big. About that time, the guessing was over. Mom rolled in my brand new huffy bike! Here is what you need to understand about most of my childhood. I did not have all the toys and games that most kids had, and I did not need all that. My first love was my skateboard, and then my bike. It was a love affair that somehow brought some form of peace and sanity into my not so peaceful, and somewhat insane, little world.

I could not believe my eyes. As a child, you are not thinking about how can they afford this? Will they be able to pay the other bills? Can they still make the car payment? The only question I had in my mind was how long it was going to take me to change out of my pajamas and into my play clothes so I could ride my new bike. In a child's world, I am sure it felt like a lifetime.

Somewhere between that Christmas and summer, the three of us moved back to Papa and Granny's house. Papa and Granny were planning a three week trip to Arkansas, and at the very last minute, Jimmy and I decided to go. Mom gave us each $20 and said she would see us when we got back. So, we hopped in the car and started our drive across country.

So, I fast-forward a little to when we got back to California from our three week trip to Arkansas. We walk into the house and somehow end up in mom's bedroom. On the pillow was a note saying she had gone to Kansas and would come back for us boys when she got settled in. I don't remember what our reaction was at the time. As a kid, I can only imagine that I just wanted to get on my bike and ride like the wind.

So, now we are back where the story started. I don't know how much time had elapsed from our trip to this day. But there was Jimmy standing in front of me crying his eyes out. I just could not understand what he was talking about and why he would be crying over my bike. Then he continued with even more tears. "They took my stereo, and now they are taking your bike. Papa says you have to come home now." One thing I learned at a very young age is that when Papa said to do something, he better not have to say it more than once. After that, the belt would do the talking. So, I hopped on my bike and pedaled as fast as my legs would take me. Had I known what was in store, I probably would have walked the bike home or taken the long way around the corner. As I got closer, I noticed a big truck out on the street in front of the house. It looked like a moving truck and had all kinds of things in the back. I wondered who was moving. When I arrived, I saw Jimmy's stereo sitting on the back of the truck, and I finally realized these were the guys who took his stereo. I wanted to pop a wheelie and knock out their teeth with my front tire.

I remember these details like it was yesterday. Papa came up to me and said those words I knew he was going to say but just did not want to hear. "Michael, you have to give these guys your bike." That's when my tears started. How could this happen to me? Did I do something wrong? I don't even remember those mean guys putting my bike on the truck and driving away. I don't remember much of anything that day. What I do remember is the very next day, Papa took me to the store and bought me a new Huffy. The child who would never be allowed in Papa's house was now having his heart mended. It was the first time I can recall having my heart torn into pieces, but I was sure thankful for my Papa.

Now here is some irony. The day after Papa bought my new bike, I left it unattended as I went into the Thrifty Store. There is another story behind this, but I will save you the details. However, my bike was stolen when it was just a day old! I should have known then that life was going to be tough!

As I look through my rearview mirror on this event, I see the role it has played in my life and how it has defined my character. Although this event was never intentional on my mom's part, she never even knew this happened until just recently. However, it is one of those defining moments in my life that has made me into the person I am today. I believe my deep roots of honor and integrity stem from this very moment in my life. Because of those deep-rooted values, I was able to pass them along to my son as well.

I recall Mike Jr. having a school project when he was in about the third grade. The project was to identify someone of great importance in their life and the reason why they chose this person. It was called the Hero Project. Once the Hero Project was completed, Mike Jr. was to give it to the person he chose as his hero.

I am not sure when the project was due or even when it was completed. However, one night I had to plan for a training exercise, and got home very late. Everyone had already gone to bed. On the dinner table I saw a sheet of paper with the words "Hero Project" written on the top. It looked something like this:

Hero Project
by Michael Miller

Who is your hero? My dad is my hero.
Why is that person your hero? Because when he makes me a promise, he always keeps it.

I never realized how much of an impact that my promises made on his life at such a young age. As I look back, I have to believe that the events like having my bike repossessed played a huge part in defining that part of my character. Even at his age, Mike Jr. knew that if I said I would deliver, he could plan on me delivering. I was his hero, and all it cost me was a bike. I think I got the better end of that deal!

Chapter 6

Shoot for the Moon!

Guiding Principle: Put some legs on your dreams.

> *What a person believes is not as important as how a person believes.* ~Timothy Virkkala

For the most part, I think we are all dreamers. Think back to when you were a kid sitting in a boring class. You found yourself staring off into space just dreaming. For many of us, this started us thinking about what we wanted to be when we grew up. If we look back on those moments in those classrooms, how many of us are really living that dream? Dreams are great. However, the dream is simply a dream. We can dream our entire lives, but if we don't put actions behind the dreams, they will simply be dreams. I once heard someone say a dream is a goal without legs.

We are all going to face challenges. However, wouldn't it be nice to eliminate as many challenges as possible? To clarify, I'm not talking about making life boring. I'm simply talking about eliminating those tedious tasks and challenges that fill our daily lives. One way to limit the number of challenges we have in our lives is to set goals. Setting goals is the easy part. Living those goals is the tough part. You see, it is not just about setting goals – it's about setting goals in better harmony with your values.

Goals offer a host of benefits, and the ones that impress me the most are goals that provide a destination. How do you know where you're going in life if you don't have a destination? Most of us spend more time planning our weekend holiday or party than we do our own lives. We don't plan to fail, we simply fail to plan.

In the previous chapter, I mentioned my trip from California to Arkansas. I don't remember a whole lot of the details of the trip, but I felt like I spent a lifetime in the car. I'm sure we stopped at a hotel every night, but I just don't remember it. But there is one thing that I do remember about those three day trips. I remember opening my eyes and realizing that the car was not moving. It was still dark, which meant it was late at night or early in the morning. I sat up in the backseat looking out the window. The car was parked on the side of the road, and my grandfather was in front of the car just looking up at the sky. I did not realize that this would become an every-morning ritual.

I got out of the car on the passenger side and walked towards my grandfather. "Papa, what are you looking at?"

Papa replied, "Do you see that really bright star out there son? It's the brightest star in the sky. That's the Morning Star, and it is thousands and thousands of miles away." He continued, "Now look at the moon. It seems further away than the stars." It was at this moment he taught me one of the most valuable lessons I have ever learned. He said, "Son, you can be anything you want to be in this world. Just set your goals high and work as hard as you can to achieve them. Remember, shoot for the moon, and if you fall short, you're still among the stars."

Are you a dreamer or a goal setter? I think most of us are dreamers. As a matter of fact, I believe only 10% of the people in this world are goal setters. So, how does one grow legs on their dreams? Set some goals and start working towards achieving those goals.

Here are some tips on how you can go from a dreamer to an achiever:

Make a decision. It's not that easy. You will probably spend more time in the valley than you will on the mountaintop. You will be faced with challenges. You will be faced with adversity, but you have to decide, and the choice is all yours. As you are setting those goals, make a decision early on that, no matter what, you will achieve that goal. Don't let anything come between you and your goal. Make the choice that your dream will become the Olympic sprinter of all dreams.

Know your values. Once you've made the decision to work towards your goals, you need to keep this in mind. If your goals are not in harmony with your values, you will fail. More difficult than setting goals is knowing and living your values. You need to do some soul-searching. You need to have core values in your life that are uncompromising. This will be a struggle for many of you because most of us live certain values because that's how we were raised. It's time to reevaluate those values. I'm not saying they're wrong, I'm just saying they may have changed. Unless we know one way or the other, we will never reach our true potential.

Define your goals and values. That's right. You have to write them down. Don't write them on a napkin or scratch paper. Don't use your lunch bag as an excuse "to go green." Find a notebook or open a clean file on your computer and start writing or typing. Make sure you have allocated plenty of time, as this will require some serious soul-searching. If you're not going to take this serious, then don't do it at all. This is serious. This could change how you live the rest of your life.

A deeper look. If you write down your goals and values, take some time to define them. What do they mean to you? Who else will they affect? What is the end result? Will you be a better person, parent, child, and friend? Will the way you live make a difference in someone else's life? Let the answers to these questions be the definitions of your goals and values.

Grow some legs. So far, we've only written down dreams. Now we need to grow legs on the dreams. Create an action plan for success. What tasks or activities will you need to perform to meet these goals? Establish milestones and reward yourself for the small victories.

Failure is not an option. I feel strongly about this statement. I feel so strong about this statement that I actually have it printed on many of my shirts. Let me explain what I mean by failure. When I say failure is not an option, I am referring to ultimate failure. Anytime we try anything new in our life, we're going to fail. When we fail, we need to learn from the failure and not make the same mistakes again. You do not need to let failure be a barrier to your success. We keep on trying. Ultimate failure can only happen when we quit. You will never reach your goals if you quit. You will never grow professionally or personally if you don't take risks in life. I recently heard a quote that is very appropriate. "Twenty years from now when we look back on our lives, we will have more regret for the risks we did not take than those risks that we did take." The number one reason that we fail is because we give up. Ultimate failure is not an option.

Don't give up. The very first step is setting goals. In the beginning, it's easy to say that we will not let anything distract us or keep us from achieving our goals. However, what we are faced with in our daily struggles in the battle seems too fierce. This is when our true character is defined. You could throw in the towel. That's probably what everybody is telling you to do anyways. Or you can be part of that 10% that does not give up. This is why you define your goals and values. During these battles, go back and revisit what you wrote. Gain your strength and live to fight another day. Do anything and everything that you must, but do not give up.

Own the possibility. Anything is possible. We have been told that all of our life. However, believing it is not enough. We have to put some action into our belief. Doing is believing. Even the Bible states that "faith without works is dead." You can have dreams and goals, but until you kick start them with actions, they are simply words – words that define someone else. Do you believe in something? Are you passionate about that belief? If so, own it or somebody else will.

Are you tired of dreaming and not living? Look forward and not back. Focus on what's ahead of you and let your past be your past. You can't change what happened ten years ago. You can't change what happened a year ago. You can't change what happened yesterday. You can't even change what happened a second ago. What you can change is your "right now." You can change your tomorrow. It may take you twenty years to reach "your moon," but twenty years is better than never reaching it at all. Should you reach the end of your life and realize you never achieved that ultimate goal, you are still a star if you gave it your all. You will have become a better person. You will have made a difference in someone's life. That will be your legacy.

The SMART Approach

Specific (dates, numbers, times, etc.)
Measurable (thinking about end result)
Attainable (conscious about the feasibility of the aim)
Relevant (relating own life with the aim)
Trackable (tracking progress of the goal)

Chapter 7

Blessings in Disguise

Guiding Principle: Some days you are the dog, and other days you are the fire hydrant. When you get the opportunity, be ready to choose. Don't let the choice be made for you.

> *Being good is commendable, but only when it is combined with doing good is it useful.* ~Author Unknown

It was freezing cold. Once again, we're on a road trip. This time it was from Kansas to Arkansas in the middle of the winter. We were traveling in an old pickup truck. There were four of us on a trip, so Jimmy and I were stuck riding in the back, and mom and Dan (not his real name) were in the front. We were curled up in our sleeping bags trying our best to protect ourselves from the cold winter wind. I remember taking the sleeping bag and zipping it up all around me. That lasted for about 30 seconds before claustrophobia sank in. I felt trapped. I began to scream as I unleashed violent punches into the sleeping bag trying to create an escape route. Jimmy managed to calm me enough to unzip my sleeping bag and free me from my prison. The cold wind on my face was much better than the claustrophobic battle I would eventually lose to the sleeping bag.

Once again, the details of this trip escape me. There must be something about non-moving vehicles that seem to wake me from a dead sleep. The truck was pulled off on the far side of the shoulder, and it must've been late at night because there was not much traffic. I peered into the cab and saw my mom in the passenger seat, but Dan was nowhere to be seen. I am not sure how much time passed, and I really didn't care. The only thing I was certain of at that time was the fact I was beginning to thaw out. I crawled back into the sleeping bag and must've dozed off to sleep.

I recall waking up to the image of a tow truck pulling up and parking in front of our broken down truck. As the driver side door opened, I remember thinking to myself, "Man, we sure are lucky this guy saw us and stopped to help." Then the passenger door opened, and Dan stepped out. What a great guy Dan was. Our truck was stranded on the side of the road, and Dan had gone on his own to get help.

The tow truck driver was very friendly and had a smile on his face that made me believe everything was going to be alright. He told all four of us to hop in the cab of the tow truck to stay warm while he hooked up our truck. I don't remember anything else that happened on the trip. I don't remember where the truck was towed to. I don't remember how long it took to repair the truck. I don't even remember riding in the back of the truck for the remainder of the trip. All I remember is thinking how Dan and the tow truck driver became instantaneous heroes in my book.

When I became a teenager, I looked back on that incident, and Dan's status went from hero to zero. What kind of man would put two little boys in the back of a truck in the middle of winter with just a sleeping bag, and begin a 500 mile journey in the middle of the night? When I think of that night and Dan's actions, there are a few not so nice phrases that come to mind. However, I choose not to dwell on the negative. I think about our friendly tow truck driver and the comfort he brought me that night.

Every other time in my life when I have needed roadside assistance, it has been a nuisance. It's just one of those things that we dread. However, when it happens to me, or I see someone on the side of the road, I am reminded of that night when I was given my blessing in disguise.

The Minister and His Wife

They were breaking the speed limit on I-65 North. They were rushing to the Louisville Children's Hospital. It was an emergency, and they could not get there quick enough. The minister and his wife had been working in missions their entire lives, but in the past year, they felt called to do a work that was completely different than what they were used to. They were not going back overseas to start a church or build a school. They were not heading to a Communist country to bring the Message to those who were being persecuted. They were not travelling around the country evangelizing. They were not going to be youth pastors or Sunday school teachers. They were going to be missionaries at the local hospitals.

In the past year, they had received several calls from the hospital chaplain or someone from the administrative staff. They had been called in to pray for a man who was terminally ill and only had days to live. They brought communion to the sick. They counseled children who were waiting for their parents to go through a major procedure. They were often present as the lonely young girl gave birth to her child. The list goes on. They had been called for a number of different reasons, but this was the first time they had received this kind of call.

It was a normal Saturday evening for them. They had just returned from dinner and were settling in for the night when the phone rang. The wife answered the phone. The minister did not have to hear the conversation on the other end of the line. It was apparent on his wife's face. She hung up the phone and said, "We have to leave now. I will explain in the car."

She took about five minutes to explain the situation. When they arrived, they met with the chaplain who asked them to wait in the lobby for their "visitor." They did not know what this visitor looked like. The chaplain said he had the visitor's name and said they would know him when they saw him. About a half an hour later, the stranger walked in with a small suitcase and swollen red eyes. They walked up to the stranger, introduced themselves, and asked if there was anything that they could do for him. Before the stranger had an opportunity to answer, the minister took him in his arms. They both wept. After a few moments, the stranger pulled away from the embrace and made this one request, "Please, take me to my kids."

The minister and his wife escorted the man to the chaplain, who then escorted him to the Intensive Care Unit. The man does not know how long the couple waited on his arrival. The man did not know when the couple actually left. All he really knew was they were two complete strangers who were there to help and provide support for a dad who had received the worst phone call a dad could receive. That man who walked into the hospital with a suitcase and swollen eyes was me. I am so thankful that God called them to provide a service to the broken and distressed.

Every positive thing in your life represents a single unique
blessing. Every negative thing in your life has the
opportunity to become a double blessing. For when you
turn a negative into a positive, you gain twice. You are
no longer burdened with the negative situation,
and in addition to that, you are strengthened by a
new positive force. ~Ralph Marston

Count Your Blessings!

Count your blessings instead of your crosses;
Count your gains instead of your losses.

Count your joys instead of your woes;
Count your friends instead of your foes.

Count your smiles instead of your tears;
Count your courage instead of your fears.

Count your full years instead of your lean;
Count your kind deeds instead of your mean.

Count your health instead of your wealth;
Love your neighbor as much as yourself.

Author Unknown

Chapter 8

Paying Forward

Guiding Principle: Be a generous giver – not because you reap what you sow, but because it just feels good!

> *We can do no great things, only small things with great love.* ~Mother Teresa

Every year, our family takes at least one vacation. Normally, that entails going to the beach, amusement parks, or other risky adventures. With three boys in our life, the vacation must be fun, or we might as well just stay at home. Two years ago, we decided to change it up a little bit. We decided to take a vacation in the Midwest. We started in Chicago, did a short stint in Indiana, and ended up our final destination in Elizabethtown, Kentucky (Mike Jr.'s home). It was probably one of the most boring vacations the boys have ever been on, but we all learned one of the most important lessons of our life that summer.

We woke up that particular morning and decided to go to Cracker Barrel for breakfast. In a small town, our choices were limited. We walked in and gave the hostess our name, and a short time later we were escorted to our table. Seated at the table behind us were two young men – probably in their mid to late 20s. There was nothing special about these two guys. They were quiet and kept to themselves.

Our family didn't do anything out of the ordinary that morning. We placed our orders and carried on as usual. We talked, joked with each other, laughed, and took turns playing the pyramid game (the one with the plastic golf tees). Our family is extremely competitive, and we were all trying to beat the other person's score. The food came, and the normal conversation and joking continued. Little did we know how our lives were about to be transformed.

I guess the guys behind us had finished their meals and had given their check because they were standing up and getting ready to leave. The man closest to us looked at my wife and said, "You really have a wonderful family."

Not expecting this, we were taken by surprise and gave the first response that came to our mind – the Elvis Presley response: "Why thank you, thank you very much." As they walked away, the rest of us were looking at each other wondering what just happened. Did we do something to generate that kind of response? We all came to the same conclusion: we were just being ourselves.

About five minutes later, our waitress approached our table and asked us if we knew those two guys. With the exception of Mike Jr., we were visitors to the small town. Our life transformation took place as the waitress spoke these words. "Those guys are not from around here either. They do travel very often though, and when they pass through Elizabeth-town, they always stop in here to eat. I normally see them about once a month." She continued, "I don't know what y'all did, but they sure like your family. They paid for your meal and would not let me tell you until they left."

Immediately, my eyes welled up with tears. I did a good job of holding back the tears, but my wife let the tears flow. For the life of us, we could not understand what we did to deserve this random act of kindness from two people we had never met in our lifetime. Out of all the people in the restaurant, why did they choose us? We will probably never know the answer to that question. We told the waitress the next time she saw those young men to thank them from the bottom of our heart. That gesture, probably very small to those guys, was a huge catalyst in changing our lives. The transformation didn't happen the following week, month, or year. It was an instantaneous life-changing moment. Neither one of us could hardly wait for the opportunity to replicate this random act of kindness. We wanted to make someone else feel exactly like we were feeling. If everybody felt like this, we could change the world!

Our opportunity came the following morning at the local Denny's restaurant. An older gentleman wearing a World War II Veteran's hat came in and sat alone. We paid his bill and slipped out before he had a chance to thank us. I am sure the same questions were going through his mind that we had going through our mind 24 hours ago. The only downside to this act of kindness is that you normally do not get to see the end result – the recipient's reaction. However, that's also what makes it so awesome. Giving is contagious and addictive. When you know how it feels to be a recipient of a random act of kindness, you want to share that with the world. You just can't do it enough.

Everywhere we go now, our eyes are open to the opportunity to be kind. We have been fortunate, though, to see some of the recipients' actions. One of those occasions happened last year in a Red Lobster here in Phoenix. We were having dinner with some friends, and within a couple of minutes of being seated, a soldier (dressed in fatigues) accompanied by his wife sat at the table directly behind us. Immediately, my wife and I locked eyes, and she nodded as to say, "Here is our opportunity to show kindness and gratitude."

It just so happened that the soldier and his wife received their meals before we did. I could see that they were almost done eating, so I motioned for our waiter. Even though we were seated directly behind each other, we had different waiters. I told our waiter our plan, and he communicated that plan to the soldier's waiter. When the soldier asked for his check, we heard his waiter say, "Sir, your meal has been taken care of by another customer in this restaurant. They wish to remain anonymous and just wanted to thank you for your service."

The soldier and his wife were rendered speechless for a moment. When he did finally speak, he said, "Tell them thank you and God bless them."

Minutes later, the soldier and his wife left, still talking about what just happened. Our waiter brought us both checks, and I handed him my credit card. As he walked away to process the credit card, the other waiter who had waited on the soldier's wife came to our table. He said, "I have never seen anything like it before in my life. I have been waiting tables for 10 years, and that is the most extraordinary thing I have ever witnessed. Thank you for allowing me to be part of. I will never forget it."

I could go on and on and tell story after story about these kinds of experiences. I could probably write an entire book about it, but my fear is that it would send the wrong message. You see, my wife and I are not looking for accolades or a pat on the back. Our goal is to simply change people's lives. If we were looking for glory and honor, we would remove the "anonymous" part of the act. We realize we are not just changing the lives of the recipients, but to those also who witness the act. We have seen a change in our own boys. They now look for opportunities to help other people who cross their paths. Here is another story that just happened last Friday.

A Cup of Water Will Do

My wife and I were on our way to our son's football game last Friday night. Lisa had volunteered to help collect the entrance fee and stamp hands. We had to arrive an hour early, and since we were running behind, we decided to grab some fast food on the way to the game. We decided to go to Wendy's since it was close to the school. As we pulled into the parking lot, we noticed it was not busy at all and decided to go inside and eat.

We walked in. There were only two other people in front of us. I'm not sure what was going on in the kitchen, but we waited for 10 minutes until we could place our order. While we waited, the line grew longer and longer. Orders were getting messed up, and both the customers and the employees were becoming very frustrated. We finally received our order and moved to the condiment bar to get ketchup and napkins. We overheard the girl behind the cash register ask the guy who was standing behind us in line how she could help him. He replied, "Can I just have a cup of ice water?"

My wife and I both turned around at the same time and noticed this man was homeless. He was so kind and patient, and it just touched our hearts. Lisa said, "Do you think he's hungry?"

I replied, "I'll ask." He came over to where we were standing, and this is how the conversation went:

> Me: "Sir, are you hungry?"
> Him: <slight pause> "Uh, yes I am."
> Me: "Would you like for us to buy you some food?"
> Him: "That would be very nice."
> Me: "What would you like?"
> Him: "The cheapest thing on the menu."
> Lisa: "Oh no! You get anything you want."
> Him: "That is so very kind of you. This caught me off guard, and I was not sure how to answer. By the way, my name is Robert, but my friends call me Bobby."

So, Bobby and I went and stood in the back of the line. My food was at the table, and we were running short on time. I opened up my wallet, pulled out a $10 bill, and gave it to Bobby. I told him we were in a hurry, and that I could not wait in line. Bobby said, "I will bring you the change."

With tears in my eyes, I said, "Bobby, just keep the change so you can have breakfast in the morning."

I will never forget Bobby's response. "Thank you, Mike, and please thank your wonderful wife. I hope that one day I will be in the position where I can help somebody like you have helped me today."

There were probably a half a dozen people standing in line witnessing this random act of kindness. Perhaps they could care less about what they just witnessed. Maybe they were just too frustrated to care. Maybe they were thinking this was another homeless alcoholic looking for a handout and was going to take the change to buy more booze. Guess what? Lisa and I didn't care what the others thought. We felt like we made a small difference in Bobby's life. We felt good about what we did. More importantly, we hope and pray that Bobby's "strong finish" is one day closer as a result.

A few years ago, Joe was at the water company taking care of some business. The lady in front of him was at the counter and begging that her water not be turned off. She was a single mother with four children and could barely put food on the table for her family. It was obvious that the person behind the counter was used to hearing these kinds of stories and simply said there was nothing he could do. She needed to come up with the money by the end of the day, or her water would be cut off. With tears running down her face, the lady gathered up her paperwork and left the building.

Joe walked up to the counter. Before the employee even had a chance to greet him, Joe asked, "How much does that lady need to keep her water on?" The guy was reluctant to share that "personal" information with Joe, but he finally did. Joe opened his checkbook and wrote a check right there on the spot.

The employee behind the counter did not know how to respond. He said, "You don't even know this lady. Why would you help her?"

Joe replied, "Because someone once helped me, and this is what Jesus would want me to do. This is my way of making a difference."

The employee said, "Sir, you have no idea how many times I hear that same story every day. You can't possibly make that much of a difference."

Joe, the starfish thrower, replied, "Well, I made a difference for that one."

It doesn't take much to make an impact in somebody's life. More times than not, we will not even see the transformation. The fact is, most of the time change happens when we are not looking.

Project Generosity

Recently, Matthew Klonowski, a board co-chairman for the Heart for the City, wanted to get a better feel of what it would be like to be in need of some of the services that the organization offers. As a result, he decided to spend time as a panhandler. Following is a description of his day:

> As I parked my car and walked to the corner that I had chosen to be "my corner," Thomas and I-17, the knot of anxiety in my stomach completely drove out the hunger that had been lodged there. I tend to do the things that most don't think of, or don't want to do, and that was why I had volunteered myself for this task. I know that the people we help don't want sympathy, and I also know that we could serve them better if we have empathy for what they are going through. As I settled myself in and held up my sign, I thought of

a quote by Guillaume Apollinaire, a French poet of the early 20th Century:

> *"Come to the edge," he said.*
> *They said, "We are afraid."*
> *"Come to the edge," he said.*
> *They came, he pushed them.*
> *And they flew....*

I smiled inwardly, hoping that I would fly and not simply fall off the edge!

It wasn't long before I realized that the knot of anxiety was fear – pure and unadulterated. I immediately began to pray for the strength to do this – to be able to live out a life that I had never before ventured into. The first minute crept by, acting as though if it went slow enough it would go unnoticed. I checked my watch. It still had consisted of only sixty seconds, even though it had seemed like a hundred! As minute number two introduced itself to my reality, I began to question what I was doing. The funds I raised – and as though my life depended on it, I truly hoped I would raise some funds – would be donated to the Heart for the City. But what if I didn't raise any funds? Worst yet, I thought, what if my next meal depended on what I raised, and I didn't raise any?

Before I had to ponder that thought for very long, a young lady in a white pick-up whipped out $2.00 and hollered, "Here!" As I walked over to get the money, I discovered that I could no longer contain my emotions, and as a result, I wept openly. As the day wore on, I became even more emotional as people gave to me – some people who obviously had little enough for themselves. The gifts of generosity that I was receiving, however, drove home the words found in Acts 20:35: "it is more blessed to give than to receive."

I kept at it, learning more than I had ever expected. More than once, I felt like quitting, but I had committed myself to this activity, and I have always maintained that commitment has nothing to do with feelings. After about two hours into it, an undercover police officer drove up and asked me if I was hungry. When I assured him that I was, he handed me a half eaten doughnut. Without hesitation, I wolfed it down in front of him. I was serious, I was hungry!

At twelve noon, after four of the most enlightening hours of my life, I called it a day. I was completely exhausted, both mentally and physically. Returning home, I ate a large meal and then took a two-hour nap. Later than evening, I evaluated what I had learned.

Being on the street, even for that short period of time, I felt completely vulnerable. To hold up that sign asking for money made me swallow every bit of pride that I had. I was scared – scared that I wouldn't raise any money at first, and then scared that someone might come by and forcibly take away from me that which I had raised. I felt lonely – and all alone, as though no one else in the world cared who I was or what happened to me. The only relief in all of this dismalness was the discovery and reality that some people, at least, had proven to be generous, even if their generosity proved to be sacrificial. The experience enforced what I already knew and felt – it is our responsibility to be generous and help those in need, even if that generosity has to be sacrificial.

Examples of Random Acts of Kindness

1. Open the door for another person.
2. When visiting a hospital, spend a few moments with someone who doesn't have any visitors.
3. Collect can goods for a food bank.
4. Clean up litter on a street in your neighborhood.
5. Say something nice to everyone you meet today.
6. Leave a kind note for a family member or friend.
7. Tell kids why you love them.
8. Visit a senior center.
9. Bring water to the homeless.
10. Say "bless you" to a stranger on the bus.
11. Put your spare change in the Ronald McDonald collection bin.
12. Pay the toll for the person behind you.
13. Put change in the parking meter you notice is getting low.
14. Leave change in the vending machine.
15. Help someone change a flat tire.
16. Tip the waitress a little more than usual.

Chapter 9

What's up Fellas?

**Guiding Principle: Showing up is the easy part.
Earning the right to be heard is the challenge.**

> *The purpose of life is not to be happy – but to matter,
> to be productive, to be useful, to have it make some
> difference that you have lived at all.* ~Leo Rosten

What defines Joe? It used to be weight lifting. He loved the challenge of working against himself, of meeting his body's limitation and pushing it further. He enjoyed the discipline of understanding the body and the muscles and how they work together. He also enjoyed the results, a well-built toned body. Now, what defines Joe is Christ and his passion for kids. Joe has always loved kids. His passion drove him to start a foundation called Heart for the City (www.heartforthecityaz.org). As a former pastor, Joe believes you should take the church to the people instead of depending on the people coming to the church. This is the same Joe who pays people's water and electrical bills.

Joe looks for ways to share Christ in a casual, non-threatening manner. In his younger days, he would go to a park to hang out and play basketball with gang members from 9:00 P.M. to 1:00 A.M. These gang members ranged in ages from 12 to 45 years old. Prior to an activity such as basketball, many of us take a few minutes to stretch and tighten our shoe laces. These gang members would take the time to empty their pockets of knives, chains, drugs, etc., and place them beside their guns along the courtside. Even in a time of leisure, their minds never wandered from survival mode. The game was very physical, and Joe had to play just as physical. Luckily, he is a big, muscular man, and this wasn't a problem. He earned their respect by playing their type of basketball and continuing to come back to play.

One night, there was an altercation with a father and a brother who came to the park to pick up their daughter/sister (a heroin addict) from another gang member. Unfortunately, the father and brother were drunk and were making threats they could not back up. The gang picked up their weapons and surrounded the father and brother with the intention of killing them. Joe wedged his way to the center of the group and said those three words that have grown to be his infamous introduction: "What's up fellas?" The same guys who had played basketball games with him had begun to place Joe on the side of the father and daughter. They had business to take care of, and nobody was going to come between them and that business – not even Joe.

But Joe continued. He said, "I know some of you have wives or girlfriends at home who love you. Some of you have a mother and nana who worry about you and love you more than anything in this world. Some of you have a sister or a brother who looks up to you as their hero and thinks you walk on water." As Joe spoke these words, he looked into their eyes. He had earned the right to be heard, and they were actually listening.

With a shaky voice and tears running down his face, he continued. "I also know that Jesus Christ loves you even more than they do. He wants to heal your pain, and he wants you to know that he loves you so much that he died for you." He didn't share very much that night, but it was enough for them to hear, and it melted their anger. They disbursed that night without any further violence. I do not know what became of those two men. What I do know is that they were given an opportunity to live another night. More importantly, they were introduced to Jesus Christ.

Joe's life is defined by his love for kids and Christ. He is a champion for any kid, any color, any race, and any cultural background. The kids without the usual advantages are his focus. Just because a kid is born on the wrong side of the tracks shouldn't mean they shouldn't have the same advantages as any other kid. He has coached high school baseball for nine years in an inner city school – a school that has never had a successful baseball program. He started with freshmen and began teaching them the game of baseball. When asked if he could start a summer program, he was told that there would never be enough kids interested in playing. Even if he had enough kids, they would not be able to afford to play. The first summer, thirty kids came out to play in the American Legion baseball league. The Anthony Holly Foundation (www.anthonyhollyfoundation.org) and the American Legion Post #29 provided the funds that made the summer program a success. The measure of success is not measured in wins and losses. Success is measured by people and organizations who have never met these kids and their families, yet are willing to partner with organizations like Heart for the City who can help.

They had many unsuccessful seasons if you keep score the traditional way, by numbers. However, Joe put time and interest into these boys and shared Christ with them. Whenever they had trouble at school or home, they went to Joe for an understanding heart and good advice. He works to see that the boys stay in school and complete their education, and even further their education. When asked what it takes to be successful with these kids, Joe's response is, "Just show up. After you show up enough times, these kids know you are there to stay and really care. Now you have earned the right to be heard."

Through the years, Joe has had many success stories. As we all know, with successes comes failures, and Joe has experienced his fair share of failures as well. As I am writing these words, Joe is burying one of "his boys" who was recently shot and killed. This is not his first funeral and will not be his last. With each funeral, he buries a piece of himself. Then, while he remembers the pain, he moves forward with a renewed focus toward reaching other kids. Joe believes we can change a community one life at a time. Those kids are his starfish on the beach. Joe is a starfish thrower.

Chapter 10

Play Like It's Your Last Game

**Guiding Principle: Talent will only take you so far.
Then you will need to depend upon your heart to
kick in and take over.**

> *"... I firmly believe that any man's finest hours –
> his greatest fulfillment of all that he holds dear –
> is that moment when he has worked his heart out
> in good cause and lies exhausted on the field
> of battle – victorious."* ~Vince Lombardi

If you are an athlete, you understand the determination and drive it takes to get to the next level – no matter what that level may be. To succeed as an athlete, you have to throw your entire life into that sport. When your friends are off having a good time, you are training and fine tuning your skills. So, of course it is just natural to get burned out at times. It is natural to step on the field and just not give it your all. It's natural because we believe we will always have tomorrow. Allow me to introduce Eriquez. (His first name is

Michael, but we all call him by his last name because there are too many Michael's in the house.)

When Kim was five months pregnant, the ultrasound technician found there was an irregular heart beat with the baby. Joe and Kim's pediatrician recommended they seek advice from a specialist. They sought out a pediatric cardiologist specialist who was able to diagnose their baby while still in the womb. The result was a mitral valve stenosis and aortic valve stenosis, which meant that his two valves were too small or too narrow. There was also a flap of fibrous tissue under the aortic valve that blocked the blood flow. The doctor said that there was not much hope for their baby, and there was a good possibility he would not make it through the first few days of life or an operation. If he did survive the operation, he may not live a year. If he did live beyond a year, he would never live a normal life. Running around with the other children or playing any kind of sports would be out of the question. Just minutes prior to breaking down in the parking garage and sobbing and crying out to God, Joe told the doctor that they still believe in a God that creates miracles. "One day," he told the doctor, "you will see a miracle."

At nine days of age, Eriquez underwent his first open heart surgery to correct the valve and to attach the tissue. This is when Joe and Kim experienced the long, cold hallway for the first time. The floor, cold and shiny, did not return a reflection of confidence. How could this be happening? Joe and Kim were two healthy parents who served the Lord and had faith that God is in control. Their faith was tested as never before. They never expected to be going through such pain and agony.

The surgery was successful – at least for about two months. At a couple of months old, Eriquez began experiencing grand mal seizures. His valve openings were too narrow to permit sufficient blood flow to his brain. When he cried, the exertion would be too much for him, and he would go into a grand mal seizure. His arms would go stiff, he would arch his back, his teeth would clench, and his eyes would roll back into his head until he would pass out. His seizures would occur 10 to 12 times a day until he was 11 months old. Then he underwent his second open heart surgery.

During his second surgery at UCLA medical center, the surgeon anticipated performing the Ross Procedure, which is removing Eriquez's aortic valve and replacing it with his own pulmonary valve. His pulmonary valve would be replaced by a frozen human donor valve. God was gracious, and this extensive procedure was averted. The surgeon was able to repair the valves sufficiently to last for another four years.

Eriquez's third open heart surgery occurred when he was almost five years old. Again, the surgeon anticipated performing the Ross Procedure, and again God was merciful. Joe held his son in his arms before he was taken to the operating room. As the nurses came in once again to take him down the long, cold hall to the operating room, Eriquez became afraid and began to cry. Through the tears, he spoke the words a parent never wants to hear, "Don't let them take me Daddy. Don't let them take me." Joe felt helpless. Kim went into the operating room with him until he was under anesthesia. Their fear was great, but it was overcome by their faith. As parents, they knew that as they drove to the hospital, with what appeared from the outside as a normal healthy son, that if his heart was left in its current condition, it would eventually take his life. As he opened his arms to give his son to the doctors, Joe and Kim knew they may never drive home with him again.

The surgeon was able to repair the valves well enough for Eriquez's body to mature. The cardiologists told them that another surgery was inevitable, but not emanate. A few years ago in a follow-up visit, the cardiologist repeated the words Joe told him before Eriquez was born: "He is a miracle."

Eriquez is now 17 years of age. His doctor has cleared him to play some sports. He cannot play football, wrestle, or lift weights, but he has been able to play basketball, soccer, golf, and baseball. Eriquez played club soccer for several years until he was 14 years old. He was a starter on the high school varsity soccer team. He was not the fastest, but he was quick and had great footwork. He understood his limitations. He was quick, but his top speed was limited to short yardage because his heart acted as a governor that prevented him from producing enough blood and oxygen to go longer distances. Because of this limitation, Eriquez knew he had to play smarter, not harder. Referees and opposing coaches commented that he understood defense better than most. The coach of the state champion commented that he had never seen anyone understand defense as well as him.

Eriquez has the heart of a champion, but his physical heart creates limitations for him. You would never know it though. He was the heart and soul of the team. A few weeks ago, I was asked to give a short motivational speech to our son's soccer team prior to a tournament. Where the team stood in the current tournament rankings, they had to win 3-0 to advance to the next game. Most of the boys know

Eriquez and are aware of his heart condition. I told them the reason he played like he did every game is because he never knew when it would be his last game. So, he played with all of his heart. When he was tired and felt like he was going to collapse, he reached deeper and found the fortitude to continue.

Seconds before our boys took the field, I asked them, "How would you play today if you knew it would be the last time you played soccer at a competitive level? Go out there and play like Eriquez would play the game. If you get knocked down, get back up. If you feel like you can't take another step, push yourself and put one foot in front of the other. Leave it all on the field today." They did exactly that. They won 3-0! Eriquez makes a difference whether he is on or off the field. Eriquez started his "strong finish" before he was ever born, and continues to finish strong.

Chapter 11

Be a Hero – Cape Optional

Guiding Principle: Life has a way of teaching us huge lessons. It's the little things that make such a major difference. Look for ways to make an impact on another life.

Everybody can be great. Because anybody can serve. You don't have to have a college degree to serve. You don't have to make your subject and your verb agree to serve.... You don't have to know the second theory of thermodynamics in physics to serve. You only need a heart full of grace. A soul generated by love.
~Martin Luther King, Jr.

A Lesson in the Shoes

My wife and I were at the Phoenix Sky Harbor airport in the security line. The TSA agent had already checked our IDs and boarding passes. We moved to the closest line and began preparing ourselves to go through the metal detector. Because of my knee surgery, I was planning for a little extra time because of the additional security measures I have to go through.

The elderly couple in front of us was moving at an extremely slow rate of speed. The wife seemed to be losing her patience with the much older husband. He removed his wallet from his pocket and placed it in the bin. Next, he reached into his pocket and pulled out the car keys. Then he reached into his other pocket and pulled out his chap stick. He reached in his back pocket for his wallet and began to panic when he realized his wallet was not in his pocket. His wife became frustrated with him. By this time, there was a line of people behind us, and we had not moved an inch. With frustration in her voice, the wife said, "You already put your wallet in here. Now, take off your shoes."

The elderly man supported himself against the table and began to remove his shoes. He took his right foot and placed it against the heel of his left shoe and slipped his foot out of the shoe. He repeated the same action for his right shoe. I was only halfway paying attention to what was going on in front of me. I found myself getting a little frustrated as well, wishing this guy would hurry up.

About that time, a man from the very back of the line started walking our direction. I was thinking this guy had some serious nerve jumping the line in front of all these people. He stopped in front of the elderly man, picked up his shoes, and placed them in his bin. The elderly gentleman said, "Thank you young man. I cannot bend over and was not sure how I was going to get my shoes."

The young man said, "You are welcome," and headed to the back of the line.

I felt so ashamed. I could not believe that this man standing directly in front of me needed assistance, and I never even noticed. I felt like a heel. That young man should have picked up a shoe and knocked me over the head before placing it in the bin.

We eventually made it through security and to our gate. However, throughout the entire trip, I could not get that event out of my mind. I made a vow to myself that I would be more aware of my surroundings. I would make a conscious effort to open my eyes beyond my own little simple world. I would look for opportunities to help those who could not help themselves. Little did I know that I would get my first opportunity a few weeks later right there at the exact same airport.

I fly Southwest Airlines as much as I can. They are my airline of choice. Their customer service is second to none, and they always seem to go the extra mile to ensure they create a pleasurable experience for their passengers. The only time I do not fly Southwest is when I am taking a trip to someplace that is not a destination point for Southwest Airlines. I was a couple of round-trips short of obtaining my A-list status, so I decided to book two back-to-back, round-trip tickets from Phoenix to Las Vegas.

I had just completed my first round-trip, sitting at the gate in Phoenix waiting for the plane to arrive. There were only a few people at the gate, so I had my choice where to sit. I sat down, propped up my feet on my computer bag, and began to read. I am not sure how much time passed when I finally looked up from reading. It was getting quite noisy from all the people that were on this flight. All the seats were taken except for the handicapped seats. There was a lady sitting in a wheelchair next to the handicapped seats. She had her back to me, so I didn't really get a good look at her. I put my nose back into the book and began to read again. About five or ten minutes later, I looked up and saw the lady in the wheelchair wheeling herself to this open area. There was a row of seats in front of me, this open area where this lady sat, and maybe handicapped seats behind her. She was using her right hand to maneuver the wheelchair and her left hand to pull her small suitcase. It was completely obvious that she was struggling. I watched for about 10 seconds as she struggled to even move an inch. The people sitting in the row directly in front of me were only about four feet from this lady. I could not believe that nobody bothered to get up and help her. Now I know how that young man felt when he had to come from the back of the line to help the older gentleman with his shoes.

I put my book down, walked around the row of seats that were front of me, and approached the lady. I placed my hand on her shoulder and said, "Ma'am, do you need some help?"

She looked up at me with tears in her eyes, and it was then that I noticed that she was much younger than I had assumed. She could not have been more than 45 years old. She replied, "It's time for me to take my pain pills, and I don't have any more water. I was trying to locate a water fountain to fill up my water bottle."

Then I replied, "I believe there is a water fountain right over there by the restroom. Would you like for me to wheel with you over there, or would you like me just to fill a water bottle?"

She said, "I have been sitting in the same place for two hours. It would be nice just to move around. If you don't mind, I would appreciate it if you would push me over to the water fountain."

So, off we went. She began to tell me her story, so I took my time. She had been involved in a car accident several months ago and severely injured her back. Her doctors said that she could walk again, but she would experience excruciating pain. She continued to tell me that she had tried walking on several occasions, but it was just too painful, so she had given up. She was tired of trying and continually failing. The pain was too much to endure, especially if she wasn't seeing any progress.

By this time, we made it back to the gate. I put the wheelchair exactly where it had been when I first arrived. Then I said, "I am going to sit right here beside you. If you need anything else, I will be right here. Just ask. And for whatever it's worth, don't give up trying to walk. I believe you can do it." I sat down in the handicapped section and was the only person sitting there. I did notice that some people were watching me. I really didn't care. Shame is a powerful motivator.

A few minutes later, the lady pre-boarded. I boarded a few minutes later and noticed she was in the front seat of the cabin. She had her head down and was not paying any attention to the other passengers as they boarded the plane. Once again, I placed my hand on her shoulder. She looked up, and when she saw it was me, she smiled. I said, "The people on the plane will take really good care of you. However, I am going to sit right behind you in case you need anything at all."

I took my seat behind her. I never heard one peep from her. She was not a burden to the flight attendants, as were any other passengers. Here is the interesting part of the story. A guy came and sat in the window seat next to me. He told me how impressed he was that I helped this lady. He could not believe that no one, including himself, offered to help, and he felt ashamed. I told him it was okay and shared my own shameful story from a few weeks ago. Life has a funny way of teaching us lessons.

Maci and Tyrone

The week before the accident, Maci found out she was the recipient of the Citizenship Award. I know Maci was happy because she loved to get awards. However, I don't think she was old enough to really appreciate how important this award really is. As parents, our cup was running over with pride. Before I share with you how wonderful Maci was, and why she deserved such a distinguished award, I will tell you about the award itself.

The National Association of Elementary School Principals (NAESP) and the National Association of Secondary School Principals (NASSP) jointly administer the American Citizenship Award. Model students who receive this prestigious honor inspire and encourage other students to strive to be better citizens. There are no "official" criteria for the American Citizenship Award. Principals bestow the award on students who:

- participate in school and/or community service
- show a positive attitude toward classmates, school, and community
- display an understanding and appreciation of civic responsibility
- possess strength of character and the courage to do what is right

- promote citizenship with their school or community through other activities.

Although she could have her moments (we called them Maci Moments) when she was not the most delightful person in the world to be around, Maci always seemed to be welcome in all circles. She was one of those kids who would light up the room with her smile. Maci would be the first to befriend the new kid at school, whether it was a boy or girl. We always knew she was special, but it is icing on the cake when someone else confirms it, especially if that someone else is the school principal, teachers, and other students.

The kids' mom and I had been divorced for almost two years at this time. I was living in the Washington, DC area, and they had gone back to Elizabethtown, KY to live. Even when we were married and had the same residential address, I was either deployed to a foreign country, on a training exercise, or working long hours. I missed out on so many things in my children's lives. There were so many stories that I had not heard because I had not made myself available. I was a good provider, but my husband and dad skills were lacking. I received a number of awards while serving in the military, but I was never nominated for the Dad of the Year Award. I placed my priority in the things that really did not matter, while my family was always taking the back seat and sloppy seconds. I am a different person today. However, I still live with the guilt of "Old Mike's" past decisions.

While attending Maci's memorial service at her school days after the accident, I heard so many people speak about the kind of person she had been and how she would leave her mark on this earth. It became glaringly obvious to why she deserved such a prestigious award. However, it was probably a few years after Maci died in the car accident that I started learning some of the stories about Maci that really made her a starfish thrower. One particular story sticks out in my mind.

Lisa and I were sitting in the bleachers of Elizabethtown High School. It was a brisk fall Friday night, and we had flown in for Senior Night. Tonight, the football team seniors would be escorted by their parents onto the field and be recognized. This was Mike Jr.'s senior year of high school and the first year he played football. Because of the injuries he had sustained from the car accident, he was limited to the kind of physical activity in which he could be involved. His doctor finally cleared him to play football his senior year.

I was so proud to be walking out on that field with him. He had turned into such a great young man. After the seniors were recognized, his mom (Rhonda) and I joined Mike's stepdad and Lisa in the bleachers. Shortly after the first quarter started, Rhonda said, "There's Tyrone." I must have had a look of confusion on my face, because she asked, "I never told you about Tyrone? He loved Maci." Rhonda and I did not talk too much about Maci, but when we did, I listened intently. I wanted to learn everything I could about her. I just knew this was going to be one of those stories, and I was right.

When she said "Tyrone loved Maci," I was a little taken back. Allow me to explain. Maci was the typical American girl. She was petite, had light brown/blond hair, and blue eyes. Tyrone was just the opposite. He was black, tall, and heavyset. In our household, there was no such thing as discrimination or racism. We did not see the color of the skin, but the softness of the person's heart. Maci was an expert at reading a person's heart. Although we taught those values, there were still those in the South who still judged a person by their color. So, it would have been perfectly normal for Tyrone not to want anything to do with Maci. What Tyrone did not know is that even if that had been the case (which it wasn't), Maci would not have taken that kind of response.

Tyrone was the new kid at school. He had arrived halfway through the school year. He was in the second grade, and a black kid in a predominately white, southern school. To top it off, his family was poor. Well, Maci did what we all would expect Maci to do. She befriended Tyrone. They sat next to each other in class, played with each other at recess, and ate lunch together. Maci learned early on that Tyrone loved chocolate milk. She also learned that he never had any money to buy an extra carton of chocolate milk. So every day, Maci would ask her mom for extra money so she could get Tyrone extra chocolate milk. Although I never met Tyrone, I am sure he would have thrown himself in a den of lions to protect Maci. I also bet there is not a carton of chocolate milk consumed by Tyrone when he does not think about his little best friend.

Shef and Charlie

It's amazing how much we take for granted. We don't realize how much we use an arm until we break it and it is casted for eight weeks. Tying my shoes is a very simple task that requires no thinking whatsoever. However, several months after my knee was replaced, I had to wear shoes that I could just slip my feet into. I had lost a considerable amount of mobility and could not bend my leg enough to tie my shoes. Oh, how I complained. As I look back now, I am reminded of the quote, "I use to complain about having no shoes until I saw a man with no feet." That's where Shef comes into the picture.

I just met Shef today. The book you are reading has been with the editor for over a month now and is scheduled to be completed tomorrow. However, this story was too amazing to not make the book.

Shef came by the house to speak to my wife and I about life and disability insurance. Shef is an older gentleman who has already retired, and just loves to sell insurance. He truly believes he is providing a service that helps others, a rare quality for most people who are in sales. In the two hours we spent together, we spoke more about personal experiences than business. Shef is a great story teller, and the more he spoke, the more I was intrigued. I was amazed by how many similarities we have in life. Although I have never caught a 450 pound marlin, Shef and I both love to play golf. So, when the golf stories started, one thing led to another, and the story about Charlie unfolded.

Shef has many years of experience in putting on golf tournaments to support different charities. When you ask Shef how he got started in golf tournament fundraising, a big smile comes across his face as he shares the story.

"Well Mike, it's funny that you should ask. Let me tell you the story. My wife, Barb, is a vocalist for the McConnell Singers. They travel around performing at hospitals, retirement communities, and anywhere they are invited. Mike, she has a beautiful voice. Well, one year they asked me to put on a golf tournament to help raise some funds for the choir. It was such a success that we now

host a golf tournament every year, and it continues
to grow. That's how it started."

So, just like every successful thing, it does not take long
before word starts spreading. One day, Shef got a call from a
friend who was requesting assistance in putting together a
golf tournament to raise funds for a little boy named Charlie.
Charlie was born without any legs or arms. He had a small
"stub" in place of a leg that he used to control his wheel
chair. However, Charlie really wanted one arm to help
improve his quality of life. He was just asking for one arm.
Time after time, insurance companies turned down his
request for a prosthetic arm because they ruled it as
cosmetic and not a need. It would cost thousands of dollars
for his arm, and Charlie's parents just could not afford it.
So, this is where Shef's and Charlie's worlds unite.

When Shef met Charlie for the first time, he expected a
child who was depressed and down on life. He was surprised
to find the exact opposite. Charlie was a very energetic and
happy boy, and had a positive outlook on life. Shef was very
moved by Charlie's story and agreed to help with the golf
tournament. The tournament brought in $50,000.00 to go
towards Charlie's new arm. What a miracle! But it does not
stop here.

Shef received a call a few weeks later. It was from a doctor
who had heard of Charlie's condition and about how a
community came together and raised the funds to get
Charlie a new arm. The doctor was moved by such a show
of compassion. With his voice shaking and fighting back the
tears, Shef repeated the words from the doctor: "You don't
have to worry about this anymore. I am going to take care of
Charlie and make sure he gets a brand new pair of arms and

legs. Additionally, it is not going to cost Charlie or anyone else a dime. This one is on me."

If you are not making a difference in someone's life, it is by choice. When Shef began the planning for the golf tournament, he never thought he would come close to raising enough funds to get Charlie a new arm. Never in a million years would he have imagined that his small gesture would make such a large impact on the heart of a surgeon. I am willing to bet that other than Charlie's parents and the doctor that performed the surgeries, Shef was one of the first real hugs that Charlie was ever able to give in his life. I would take another wager and bet that there are not too many people that do not get a hug from Charlie.

Chapter 12

Small Gesture = Huge Impact

**Guiding Principle: A small thank you means more
than you can possibly imagine.**

> *The purpose of life is not to be happy – but to matter, to
> be productive, to be useful, to have it make some
> difference that you have lived at all.* ~Leo Rosten

Look around you. The veteran is everywhere. They are our
sons and daughters. They are our brothers and sisters. They
are our nieces and nephews. They are our dads and moms.
They may be the person standing a few lines over in the
grocery store. They may be in the vehicle behind you at the
drive-thru. They may be sitting a couple pews in front of
you at church. Some are recognizable by their high and tight
haircut. Others are easily identifiable when wearing their
uniforms in a public area. Some, you have to look deep into
their eyes, and there you might get a small glimpse into their
soul – a soul that will carry the weight of unspeakable
sorrow from losing a friend or having to take another life in

the name of freedom. The important thing is to open your eyes and be aware that they are all around you.

The Wal-Mart Photographer

My firstborn son was born a month before I left for Desert Storm. I was deployed for six months and watched him grow in photographs. It seemed like we could not get enough pictures of him. A couple of months after I returned from Iraq, my wife, son, and I took leave from Germany to visit my relatives in Phoenix. Our families had planned quite a few things for us, but I wanted to make sure we scheduled a picture session for our son.

After three days arriving in Phoenix, we took our son to Wal-Mart to get his picture taken. We had a coupon that allowed us to get three poses with this package. The photographer took multiple poses and told us to come back in a week. A week passed, and we returned.

The photographer had seven different poses displayed. What a salesperson! Our budget was extremely tight, as I was just a young soldier making enough to barely make ends meet. After a few minutes, I could tell my wife was struggling with the decision. After all, they looked so darn cute. She replied, "I am just having trouble deciding on three of them."

The salesperson said, "Well, buy them all."

And of course, I piped in and said, "Honey, we only can get three. You really need to decide."

She said, "Ok. Give me a couple of minutes."

While she was deciding, the photographer and I began to chat. I had a high and tight haircut, and a very dark tan from being in Iraq. He asked me if I was in the military, and I said yes. He asked me if I had been over in Desert Storm. I said yes, and that I had just got back home. We talked for just a little bit longer, then he looked at my wife and said, "I see you are having trouble deciding on three poses. If you could pick five, which ones would you pick?"

She immediately replied, "I would take that one, that one, those two, and that one." He gathered up the pictures, put them in the bag, handed them to me, and thanked me for my service to our country.

That happened 19 years ago, and to this day, I have not forgotten it. I would have gladly given up all of my medals for such a small but gracious act of kindness.

If you recognize a veteran, no matter where you are, walk up to them and shake their hand and thank them for their service. All of us soldiers take pride in our uniforms and the medals we have earned. However, a thank you from those we serve and protect means more than you will ever know. Although this story is focused on the soldier, make it a practice to thank all of those who serve on a daily basis.

Care Packages from Home

I was deployed to Iraq during the first Gulf War in 1991. Technology was nowhere even close to what it is today. We had no personal computers to email and web cam with our loved ones. We had no cell phones. We stood in line for hours just to make a 10 minute call back to the States. When the war started, that came to an end. We waited for months before our mail finally caught up to us. Mail call was the most exciting part of the week. We would stand in a group waiting for our names to be called. When our name was called, we would sprint to the front to collect our mail. For those who received mail, it was a great day. For the rest, it was a disappointment.

I recall day after day going by and never hearing my name called. My other buddies were getting mail, but I had not received any. Finally, after two months, I heard those sweet words, "Private Miller!" I ran to the front to collect my mail. I was smiling so hard that it hurt. I grabbed the envelope from the sergeant's hand, and my smile turned to a frown. My first piece of mail was a phone bill from AT&T. They must have paid extra to make sure I got their bill! Eventually, I started getting mail, and that was a huge morale booster.

There are three particular items that were sent from the U.S. that made a huge impact on my life. The first one was from a second-grader in the town where I graduated high school. It was a Valentine's Day card thanking me for serving our country and asking me to be her valentine. It was simply addressed to "Soldier," but was hand decorated and signed by this little girl. Somehow that card was lost during one of our movements, and I never had the chance to directly thank her. I hope that one day she will understand how wonderful that made me feel.

The second item was a huge box with a variety of different things. They were called care packages. People from all over the U.S. would donate goods or money. The items were placed in a large box and shipped to a unit. We opened that box to find candy, gum, wet wipes, toilet paper, writing pads, pens, Kleenex, baby powder, tooth brushes, and a number of other personal hygiene items. Once again, I was amazed by the support we were getting at home. We took some of the things that we needed, and we ended up giving the rest to a group of Iraqi children. I think they may have been happier than we were.

The last item that was probably the most important actually came to my friend, Scott. He opened up this small envelope to find two small cloths about the size of a dollar bill torn in half. On a note were these words:

> These cloths have been anointed with oil and have been prayed for by every member of our congregation. We pray that you will keep them with you, and they will protect you from all harm, and come home safely. We love you and are proud of you. God Bless you.

It was signed by a Baptist church in Georgia. Scott took one of the cloths and gave me one. We wrapped the cloth around one of our dog tags and used tape to secure it. We both wanted that prayer cloth to be as close to our heart as possible. To this day, I am sure that the prayer cloth protected me and brought me home safely to my family.

To those who have never served in combat, you may not understand how much something so small can make a difference in a soldier's life. A valentine's card, a pack of gum, and a prayer cloth impacted me so much that 20 years later I am writing about it. There are a number of organizations that you can donate to that will send a care package to a soldier. You can send messages through different websites. The great thing about the internet is that the options are unlimited. Here are some testimonials that I found from soldiers who had received a care package from home:

"I would personally like to thank all of those who have recently contributed their time and efforts in what I believe to be an awe inspiring, and frankly, quite dramatic display of support from the home-front. The correspondence and care packages have been coming in at an overwhelming, and nearly monumental, pace. The "Any Soldier" campaign has seen tears from some, given hope to most, and has been inspirational to us all. Your relentless support has provided the simple reminder that any one of us would proudly die for a grateful nation in our ongoing fight against terrorism."

"I couldn't be any more proud to have been a part of such an honorable organization as AnySoldier.com. This is priceless, and I would like to thank all of you who entrusted me to be your contact. To have been able to distribute the mail personally as a contact to soldiers who get next to no mail at all, and for that brief moment, see the look of hope in their faces of good things to come. The hope that somebody out there does care. That somebody does in fact love them as they deservingly should be loved. The hope that someday their involvement in the fight on terror was to preserve those that believed in them so much through and through, until their fight was done. We fight so that maybe, just maybe, your grandchildren won't have to. Pray for us in all that we do."

"It was a shower of blessings for our Soldiers to receive the care packages you and your team prepared and sent to us. We thank you from the bottom of our hearts for your hard work, love, and

support. There are not enough words that can express the unconditional love you have in supporting our Soldiers. We also thank you for your prayers. You and your loved ones are in our prayers as well. May God continue to enrich your hearts and bless you with good health and prosperity. Thank you and God bless."

"Thank you very much for the Care Package. It means so much to us here to receive a little taste of home every now and then. I shared some of the contents with some soldiers going through hard times and want to thank you again on behalf of them. We appreciate your kindness and thoughtfulness very much. God bless you."

Never forget, it is the little things that make a difference – even in the life of a soldier. You do not have to believe in the war to support the war fighter. You do not have to carry a weapon and travel to foreign soil to make a difference. Do something small – a heartfelt unexpected gesture – and thank God we have men and women who protect our freedoms that we so often take for granted. Freedom is not free. If you love your freedom, thank a vet.

Chapter 13

Saving Lives Incognito

Guiding Principle: Sometimes the life you think you are saving is actually saving your life.

> *Act as if what you do makes a difference. It does.*
> ~William James

It had been about six months since Maci passed, and I was still at the point where I was grasping for straws just trying to survive. During the day, I threw myself into my work. At night, I was still drinking heavily and taking prescription drugs. I had been attending Compassionate Friends meetings for several months at this point. In an effort to take my mind off of my pain and suffering, I had volunteered for several responsibilities within Compassionate Friends. I had volunteered as the newsletter editor, the membership database manager, and a hotline for dads who had lost a child.

To be quite honest, I never expected to get any calls on the hotline. After all, I expected all men to grieve just like me – be strong and keep it all in. So, you can imagine my surprise when the phone rings one night at about one in the morning. I wasn't completely asleep and wasn't completely awake either. I was kind of in that limbo stage where you feel half rested and groggy.

When the man on the other end of the line started speaking, it only took me a couple of minutes to become fully alert. "Hi, my name is Bob. I was given your phone number and was told I could call you if I needed to talk. I know it's early in the morning I had to talk to somebody." So, as we began to talk, I headed downstairs. I grabbed the bottle of Jack Daniels from atop the refrigerator and a glass out of the sink, and headed outside. The more Bob talked, the more I drank. Here is the story.

Bob had been married for seven years and had two children (a boy and a girl) and a great job. He was very successful and was climbing the corporate ladder. He had everything going for him. Then the unthinkable happened. On the way home from church one night, a drunk driver crossed the line and collided with their car. Bob's son died at the scene.

Bob's story was very familiar. We both were fathers to two children, but due to an unthinkable twist of fate, half of our world was taken from us. Our child was gone, and we never had the chance to say goodbye. One of the main differences between Bob and I was the fact that he was married, and I was divorced at the time of my loss. I often wonder what would have been our fate had we still been married. I doubt our chances would have been good. Studies show that one half of marriages end up in divorce. Those are marriages that deal with everyday normal challenges. Now let's take a look at the 50% of those marriages that do make it. It's hard work and requires an effort of both the man and the woman. Now throw in the stress of losing a child, trying to figure out how to cope, trying to be strong for your other child, and the fact that you spend the majority of your time grieving alone because you and your spouse grieve completely different. How many of those marriages do you think actually make it? I am certain that I would have been one of the statistics, and now this lonely man on the other end of the phone who not so long ago had it all going for him, had become one of these statistics. He had joined the club of the fatherless, the wifeless, and the jobless.

Bob and I talked for hours until the sun came up. There were gaps in our conversation – sometimes several minutes – as we wept. We were in survival mode. Getting out of bed every day was a victory. Going to work and being strong in the face of your colleagues was a daunting task. After all, in their minds, it was time to move on. We needed to let it go. As we ended our conversation and I hung up the phone, I realized three things immediately.

1. I had drank a considerable amount of Jack Daniels and made a mental note to stop by the liquor store on the way home.
2. I had failed to get Bob's phone number. After talking and drinking (probably more of the latter) for several hours, I completely forgot that Bob's number had come through on the caller ID as a private number.
3. I was in no position to help anybody. I needed just as much help as the next guy. I just didn't have the guts to pick up the phone and call someone.

That was the first call I had ever taken on the hot line, and I blew it. I could not believe that I did not get Bob's telephone number. The first two things I realized were not that critical. However, the fact that I needed just as much help as Bob made me more than unqualified for this position. Had I been

Bob, I would've fired me over the phone. Since Bob did not fire me, I did the next best thing. I immediately resigned. Little did I know that my hotline job would have been so short-lived. Bob was my first call and my last call.

For several months after that call, Bob periodically crossed my mind. I wondered where he was, how he was doing, and hoped he was better than I. I was approaching the one year anniversary of losing Maci. The shock of losing her was beginning to wear off, and now I began to understand why they said the second year is probably worse than the first year. The first year, I was not in control. My subconscious mind took over and used shock as a defense mechanism to survive. I guess my mind thought it was time to give me back the reins. As the shock began to subside, I felt this indescribable pain in the depths of my heart and soul.

Every Compassionate Friends meeting was a necessity for me. I needed every ounce of support from those meetings to get me through the next day. Since Compassionate Friends only met one night a month, I honestly felt that I could barely keep my head above water the rest of the month. So when I walked into these meetings, I was selfish. It was all about me. What could I glean from that meeting to carry me through? I was in survival mode.

On this particular night, I arrived about five minutes before the meeting was supposed to start. I scanned the room to see if I could find a chair next to one of the regulars. Far across the room, our chapter leader was speaking to a man I'd never seen before. This guy looked like Grizzly Adams on steroids. The chapter leader pointed my direction, and Grizzly Adams started my way. The closer he got, the larger he became. He must have been 6 1/2 feet tall and maybe 280 pounds of solid muscle. He was a giant and was coming right at me. I think I got a small taste of what David felt like when he was about to do battle with Goliath.

I began to wonder how I could possibly know this guy. Maybe I cut him off on the freeway? Perhaps I took his right-of-way at a four-way stop? Did I steal his parking place at the grocery store? Maybe he cut me off, and I gave him the one-finger salute? Was he standing behind me when I took the last bottle of Jack Daniels off the liquor store shelf? Okay, I know these thoughts sound ridiculous, but I am blaming it on my subconscious taking over my mind once again.

Here he was, right in front of me. I introduced myself and offered my hand, hoping he would not crush every bone when he shook it. He opened his mouth to speak, and with tears in his eyes, he said, "I know who you are Mike. You may not remember me, but I called you several months ago, and we talked for several hours. I'm Bob." Can you recall the thought that crosses your mind when you meet somebody for the first time and you think to yourself, "I had a completely different picture of you in my mind?" Well, that's the thought that went through my mind.

I didn't have much time to think about anything else. Before I knew it, Bob had his arms around me, and he lifted me off the ground, applying one of the fiercest bear hugs I have ever received. I remember hugging him back as my feet dangled about a foot above the ground. He put me back down on the ground, and as the tears rolled down his cheeks, he said something to me that would impact me forever. He said, "That night when I called you, I had reached the end of my road. I had a bottle of whiskey on the table, the telephone in my left hand, and my pistol in my right hand. I was going to end my life. But Mike, you gave me strength. I thought if you could make it, I could make it. I haven't made it yet, but I am making it."

In a time when I thought it was I who needed to be saved, somehow I was able to save another. You would think that would've given me strength and encouragement for my own battle. However, a short time after meeting Bob, my life headed in a downward spiral. I don't think I ever hit bottom. I just did a nosedive and busted right through the bottom. This was the loneliest and darkest place I've ever been in my life. I made decisions and choices in my life in that period of time that I am too ashamed to speak of or even write about. Eventually, I began the long, slow climb out of this pit. It was a constant struggle, and I was literally fighting for my life. Some battles were tougher than others, and it was during those toughest fights that I leaned on Bob's words – "I haven't made it yet, but I'm making it."

Bob was my starfish. He was my one and only call. I thought I had struck out, but in all actuality, I was batting a thousand. I hit it out of the park, but the true MVP was Bob. It took more guts for him to place the call than for me to answer the call. It took humility to cry, especially to another man. It took courage to set the pistol on the table and make a decision to try to fight just one more day. And in the end, it was Bob's words that gave me encouragement to fight my fight and to face my battles just one more day.

Bob, if you read this book, I am your starfish.

Rescued

We all take things for granted. It is part of our human nature. We think we can understand what other people are going through. However, unless we have personally experienced something in our lives, we cannot possibly begin to understand what it truly feels like. That is the different between sympathy and empathy. For women, child bearing is a normal part of life. It is what one of those special miracles from God bestowed on women. As most women will say, God gave that task to women because he knew a man could not handle it. However, not being able to bear children would seem indescribable to me. My sister, Heather, is one of those women. However, instead of letting it defeat her, she did something very amazing. She adopted. I think she is a hero. She gave two beautiful children the opportunity to have a life they would have otherwise never known. I asked Heather to tell her story. Here it is:

I found out in my teens that I would never be able to have children the natural way. I was born with Spina Bifida, and along with that birth defect, I had other medical issues that would make it impossible to carry a child. The news has always seemed to bother those close to me more than it did me. I decided that if I ever wanted to be a mother, I would just adopt, as I come from a blended family, and biology was never a determining factor in how much we love each other. I put the news in the back of my mind and carried on through my teenage and early adult years. It wasn't until my mid twenties that I started thinking seriously about how I wanted the rest of my life to play out. I had dated and had a few serious relationships, but learned quickly that talking about my medical issues and explaining that I wouldn't ever be able to become pregnant was always the reason those relationships ended. I knew that if I eventually wanted children, I wanted them to have two parents who were equally committed to raising them. I met my husband in 2000, and on our first date, I decided to just show all my cards and see what happened. As we made small talk over dinner, I told him about my situation, and to my surprise, he wasn't fazed at all and shared with me that his brother was adopted. We got married in 2003 and wasted no time registering with the same adoption agency that his brother was adopted from.

I don't think either one of us was prepared for the emotional rollercoaster that we would experience during the adoption process. We decided on inter- national adoption and chose Guatemala, primarily because we wanted to adopt an infant and because the children were placed with loving foster families at birth. I can honestly tell you that I fell in love the very moment I saw a picture of my son. It was a feeling that I had never experienced, and bringing him home consumed my every thought. I am not blessed with patience, and waiting to hold him threatened to do me in. We decided to visit him in Guatemala when he was about nine weeks old, and although it was awful to leave him, I am so thankful that I have those special memories. I didn't know then just how completely my life was about to change. Holding my son for the first time and caring for him on our trip was amazing. I know that it was on that trip that the softening of my heart had begun. I remember landing in Guatemala for the first time and seeing the absolute poverty around me. I also remembered that the adoption agency had stressed to us in our classes about what adoption wasn't. They made sure we knew that adoption wasn't saving or rescuing a child. As I looked around me, I wondered if they had been to the same Guatemala. We were greeted by children no more than four years old begging for money outside the airport doors. My heart just hurts when I think back to that and picture my son or daughter needing to do that for their family. We didn't get to meet the birth mothers of either of our children, but I am so grateful for the brave and unselfish decision they made for their children.

Eventually, my son came home in January 2005 at four and a half months, and we brought our daughter home from Guatemala in November 2006 at five months old. I remember the middle of the night feedings with both of them, and how I would just stare at them and cry because I couldn't believe what I had been blessed with. Both of my children have tender, caring hearts, and there isn't a day that goes by that I don't learn a lesson from one of them. They are truly a blessing to our family, and I am so honored to call them my children. I know that they will have more opportunities here than they would have had in Guatemala, but if anyone was rescued, it was me.

Where There's Smoke, There's Fire

It was December 1991, and some friends were over at the house playing cards. We were living in Nurnberg, Germany, and only had a few weeks before we would be heading back to the United States. Our entire unit had deactivated, and the entire unit was relocating to Fort Knox, KY. For those soldiers who had family members, the Army put us up in temporary housing. The temporary housing was on the top floor of the government leased apartment building – about five stories high.

It was about 11:30 P.M. when we heard someone in the parking lot yell, "Fire!" My buddy, Davis, and I both jumped to our feet and looked out the window. In the basement of the apartment building across the street, we could see flames shooting out of the windows. Without a second thought, we darted out the door and down the stairs. All I remember is hearing our wives yelling, "Be careful! Don't go into the building!"

We were taking two to three stairs at a time. When we reached the bottom, we darted across the parking lot to the front of the building. A man who obviously had too much to drink said someone had thrown a bottle with a lit rag through the basement window. The smoke was bellowing up into the apartment building, but no one was coming outside. There were no emergency vehicles in sight, and we could not hear any sirens. So, we did what anybody else would have done. We told the inebriated guy to call in the fire, and Davis and I bolted into the building.

Davis stopped at the first door he came to and started knocking and yelling. I continued to run upstairs to the top floor. I began to knock on all the doors and yelling "Fire!" People started coming out into the hallways. By that time, the smoke was getting pretty bad, so I did not need to convince anyone that this was not a prank. I told some of the men to help knock on doors and wake people up. I then started down to the next floor and continued giving the same warning.

Once again, I barked orders to the men and told them to help. I was about to head down to the third floor when a door opened up and a black lady stood there. She was crying and had a look of fear on her face. Then she said, "My husband is deployed, and I am here with my three kids. Can you please help me?"

I said, "Yes, show me to the kids' rooms."

I followed her into the room. I picked up the youngest child, which was probably about a year old. About that time, a little figure appeared in the doorway. He was probably about three or four years old. I grabbed his hand and told him to come with me. Mom grabbed the other child and followed me out the door. I told her to stay right on my tail. We made it down the stairs and out the building. Davis's and my wife were in the parking lot, and a huge expression of relief came over my wife's face when I appeared. I gave the lady the baby and turned back around to look at the building. It was obvious that there were still more people in the building.

So, I took off again. I made it to the second floor before the smoke consumed me. I removed my sweatshirt and wrapped it around my face in an effort to act as a ventilation system and help me not to take in so much smoke. I went to the second floor and met Davis. He told me that the top floors were cleared, but there were still some people on this floor. So, we continued with our warnings. We finally managed to get everyone out of the building. It was a good thing because I could hardly breathe anymore. It seemed like hours, but only a few minutes had passed. I ended up carrying two or three more kids to safety by the time it was all said and done.

As we were catching our breath, the fire truck showed up. We figured it was safe to leave, so the four of us headed back up the stairs. Obviously, that was our topic of conversation the remainder of the night. Davis and I were pumped up, and the adrenalin was running through our veins. Of course, our wives were telling us how stupid we were. We later learned that the fire was somehow contained to the basement, and the most significant danger came from the smoke inhalation. Everyone survived and was going to be ok.

Several days later, I was walking past the playground and recognized the family as the ones who I had taken from the building first. The mom recognized me and smiled. I walked up to her and asked her how the family was doing. She hugged me and thanked me for "saving their lives." She called the little boy over and said to him, "This is the man who saved us from the burning building. Tell him what you wanted to say." Of course, he was too shy and ran off to play. His mother looked at me and said, "Please don't take this the wrong way, but I wanted to tell you exactly what he said that night." She proceeded to quote her little son: "Mommy, that little white man is my hero. It's like he was a white angel that came and saved us all."

She hugged me and thanked me again. I had to turn and walk away because I did not want her to see me crying. I only hope that if that boy ever has the opportunity to help someone, he will remember his "white hero" and not even hesitate.

Had Davis and I waited around and given our reports to the authorities, I know the military would have given us a rather prestigious medal. The fact of the matter is that we did not even think about that until a couple of weeks later. By then, I had already received all the praise I needed. Me being a hero and life saver in the eyes of a child was far greater than any award the military could have provided.

So, am I saying you have to run into a burning building to be a hero? Do you have to pull someone from a wreck? Do you have to jump into the ocean and save a drowning person? You do not have to do any of these. You just have to look for opportunities to make a difference in someone's life – no matter how big or small the gesture.

Chapter 14

The Ordinary Accomplishing the Extraordinary

Guiding Principle: You do not have to be a celebrity or someone famous to make an impact. You just have to be willing.

"I shall pass this way but once. Therefore, any good that I can do or any kindness that I can show, let me do it now, for I shall not pass this way again." ~Stephen Grellet

---

Lesson From a Friend

"This guy has done it right." That was one of my first thoughts I had of Steve shortly after meeting him. I had heard numerous stories prior to meeting him, but the stories did not give him justice. I heard how wonderful of a boss he was. He is the best family man you can ask for. He has such an amazing walk with God. He is so successful. It goes on and on. I was thinking to myself that no one was that perfect. Then I met him. The more I got to know Steve, the

---

more I wanted to be a better person. He was just that kind of guy.

The one thing Steve and I had in common was our ambition and drive for success. We enjoy the finer things in life, and we worked our tail ends off to get them. In our mind, success was about making as much money as possible and providing for our family. That's a good goal to have. However, when it becomes your ultimate goal in which everything else takes a back seat, it becomes ever consuming. We have all heard stories of extremely successful people who are near the end of their life. When they look back on their lives, they do not wish they had spent more time at work. As a matter of fact, it often times becomes a regret.

When I picked up my phone and heard my wife crying on the other end, I knew the message was not good. A few days before, we received the call that Steve was going through additional tests after a routine physical. Lisa had just received the update and was calling me. "Hon, Steve got his results back. He has stage 4 cancer. They are heading home to San Antonio tomorrow and want to have dinner with us tonight." It was September 15, 2008.

As we drove towards the restaurant that night, I had positive thoughts. Steve was in amazing shape. He was only 51 years old, worked out routinely, and ran every day. Steve was a fighter. Most importantly, he was a man of God. It's cancer. So what? Steve is going to fight this and win. There are thousands of successful cancer survivors who have claimed victory. If anyone could do it, it was Steve.

We walked into a crowded Red Robin restaurant and hugged Steve and his wife, Cristol. Then they told us the specifics. Steve was diagnosed with stage 4 colon cancer and a metastasized liver. They told him that he needed to go home and get his affairs in order. Then he said those words that I will never forget. "Mike, I spent my entire life chasing the gold ring, and look where it's landed me." I was confused. How could this be? How could the man who I looked up to – who I thought was the man, the myth, and the legend – have any regrets? He did it right....right?

Steve did what every one of us does. He was looking in the past and regretting some of the decisions he made. The difference was that we still have our entire lives (at least we think we do), and Steve's life was coming to an end very quickly. In most of our eyes, Steve was perfect. Most men only aspire to be like Steve, but very few ever make it. But for Steve, he felt he could have been better. That's what made Steve such an awesome man!

Steve refused to accept that he only had a few weeks to live. As a matter of fact, Steve refused to believe that this cancer was going to beat him. He was a fighter, and he had faith in God. Steve's declaration of faith was: Psalm 118:17...*I choose to live I will not die and declare the works of the Lord.*

So the fight began. He was immediately accepted by the Cancer Treatment Center of America in Tulsa, OK, and chemotherapy began. On January 17, four months after Steve was diagnosed and three months longer than the doctors had given him to live, Cristol posted the following message on the CarePages website:

> Praise God, Steve's healing is nearly complete!! Thank you, thank you, thank you for all the prayers, because the Lord is so faithful in his promises. The PET scan showed that there was

"NO" cancer in the colon!! Thank you, Jesus!! His cancer marker count is now at "11", with "7" being the normal number for us. Although the liver was still showing some active cancer tumors....the doctor's think that they may be able to get the rest of it through some direct radiation therapy. But there is "NO CANCER" anywhere else in his body. Hallelujah!! The Dr's were very excited that this has all come so quickly. They are still baffled at how this terminal cancer has turned around in only a few short months. So, needless to say, we are dancing for JOY because we know that God will complete Steve's healing very soon. In the Name Of Jesus!!!

We had visited with Steve on one of their visits back to Phoenix, and he looked unbelievable. You would have never known that this man was battling for his life. Over the next couple of months, the cancer would raise its ugly head, but Steve still continued to claim victory. On March 22, 2009, he gave his testimony in Lexington, KY at the Mount Zion Christian Church. You can see his testimony at http://mtzioncc.com/video/service2009-03-22.html. This is a must see testimony! This is Steve's "strong finish!"

On May 15, we got word that Steve's body was no longer accepting the chemo. He began to go downhill. Lisa and I knew we needed to go to see Steve. My son graduated high school on Friday, June 5, 2009. On Saturday, June 6, we flew to Tulsa and spent two hours with Steve. That was the last time we saw Steve alive. On June 16, 2009, Steve went to meet his maker. Steve claimed healing in his testimony. God promised him healing, but instead of the physical healing we were hoping for, God healed Steve spiritually.

Steve inspired people his entire life. Steve changed lives his last eight months on earth. I know because he changed my life. Steve is no longer with us, but he left his legacy. Here are a couple of postings from CarePages:

Steve was an amazing influence in my life as a working peer and simply the best friend I've ever had in my entire life! I was always amazed by his passion for life, and his glass was not always half full, but rather over-flowing. His positive, never quit style, combined with his consistent outward love for his family and his church, were truly unwavering. Steve's friendship was completely unconditional all the time, every time! I miss him dearly and smile often when I see his picture on my desk. –Rick

When I heard Steve share the experience that he had with the Lord after he had received the news regarding his condition, I was changed. I was amazed too at the change in Steve to share with everyone he knew about making sure you are headed in the "right" direction. His honesty and integrity still inspires me today. I am thankful that the Lord allowed our paths to cross. He left footprints behind so others may find their way home to the Father. What better legacy is there than that? –Rosie

Steve's life was changed. When told to get his affairs in order, he realized he had just been going through the motions. In his testimony, he asked, "If you were given the news today that he had been given, what would you do with your life?" Steve's advice is to live right now. Make a difference today. Begin your "strong finish" now. In the words of Tim McGraw's song, "… and I loved deeper, and I spoke sweeter, and I gave forgiveness I'd been denying. And he said someday I hope you get the chance to live like you were dying."

Chapter 15

Freedom is Not Free

**Guiding Principle: If you love your freedom,
thank a vet.**

---

*"For those who fight to protect it, freedom has a flavor
that the protected will never know."*

In my opinion, there is no greater calling than serving
others. If you are fortunate enough to serve in our Armed
Forces, you truly understand the great privilege and honor
it is to serve. General Douglas MacArthur delivers one of
the best explanations of what it means to serve in the
military:

"Duty," "Honor," "Country" – those three hallowed words reverently dictate what you want to be, what you can be, what you will be. They are your rallying point to build courage when courage seems to fail, to regain faith when there seems to be little cause for faith, to create hope when hope becomes forlorn.

These are some of the things they do. They build your basic character. They mold you for your future roles as the custodians of the nation's defense. They make you strong enough to know when you are weak, and brave enough to face yourself when you are afraid.

They teach you to be proud and unbending in honest failure, but humble and gentle in success; not to substitute words for action; not to seek the path of comfort, but to face the stress and spur of difficulty and challenge; to learn to stand up in the storm, but to have compassion on those who fall; to master yourself before you seek to master others; to have a heart that is clean, a goal that is high; to learn to laugh, yet never forget how to weep; to reach into the future, yet never neglect the past; to be serious, yet never take yourself too seriously; to be modest so that you will remember the simplicity of true greatness; the open mind of true wisdom, the meekness of true strength.

He was an average kid living an ordinary life. Raised in Knox, Pennsylvania with his two sisters, Ross McGinnis signed up for the United States Army's delayed entry program at 17 years old. Upon graduating high school, he immediately went to basic training and was deployed to Iraq in August 2006. Three months later, PFC McGinnis engaged in the most selfless service act that a soldier could possibly do, and because of his heroism, was awarded the highest and most prestigious award given to any service member – The Congressional Medal of Honor. Here is how the actual citation read:

For conspicuous gallantry and intrepidity at the risk of his life above and beyond the call of duty:

Private First Class Ross A. McGinnis distinguished himself by acts of gallantry and intrepidity above and beyond the call of duty while serving as an M2 .50-caliber Machine Gunner, 1st Platoon, C Company, 1st Battalion, 26th Infantry Regiment, in connection with combat operations against an armed enemy in Adhamiyah, Northeast Baghdad, Iraq, on 4 December 2006.

That afternoon his platoon was conducting combat control operations in an effort to reduce and control sectarian violence in the area. While Private McGinnis was manning the M2 .50-caliber Machine Gun, a fragmentation grenade thrown by an insurgent fell through the gunner's hatch into the vehicle. Reacting quickly, he yelled "grenade," allowing all four members of his crew to prepare for the grenade's blast. Then, rather than leaping from the gunner's hatch to safety, Private McGinnis made the courageous decision to protect his crew. In a selfless act of bravery, in which he was mortally wounded, Private McGinnis covered the live grenade, pinning it between his body and the vehicle and absorbing most of the explosion.

Private McGinnis' gallant action directly saved four men from certain serious injury or death. Private First Class McGinnis' extraordinary heroism and selflessness at the cost of his own life, above and beyond the call of duty, are in keeping with the highest traditions of the military service and reflect great credit upon himself, his unit, and the United States Army.

Here are some of the President's remarks during the awards ceremony:

A week ago on Memorial Day, the flag of the United States flew in half-staff in tribute to those who fell in service to our country. Today we pay special homage to one of those heroes: Private First Class Ross Andrew McGinnis of the U.S. Army. Private McGinnis died in a combat zone in Iraq on December the 4, 2006 – and for his heroism that day, he now receives the Medal of Honor.

A special welcome to the prior recipients of the Medal of Honor, whose presence here is – means a lot to the McGinnis family. Thank you for coming.

The Medal of Honor is the nation's highest military distinction. It's given for valor beyond anything that duty could require, or a superior could command. By long tradition, it's presented by the President. For any President, doing so is a high privilege.

Before he entered our country's history, Ross McGinnis came of age in the town of Knox, Pennsylvania. Back home, they remember a slender boy with a big heart and a carefree spirit. He was a regular guy. He loved playing basketball. He loved working on cars. He wasn't too wild about school-work. (Laughter.) He had a lot of friends and a great sense of humor. In high school and in the Army, Ross became known for his ability to do impersonations. A buddy from boot camp said that Ross was the only man there who could make the drill sergeant laugh. (Laughter.)

Most of all, those who knew Ross McGinnis recall him as a dependable friend and a really good guy. If Ross was your buddy and you needed help or you got in trouble, he'd stick with you and be the one you could count on. One of his friends told a reporter that Ross was the type "who would do anything for anybody."

That element of his character was to make all the difference when Ross McGinnis became a soldier in the Army. One afternoon 18 months ago, Private McGinnis was part of a Humvee patrol in a neigh-borhood of Baghdad. From his position in the gun turret, he noticed a grenade thrown directly at the vehicle. In an instant, the grenade dropped through the gunner's hatch. He shouted a warning to the four men inside. Confined in that tiny space, the soldiers had no chance of escaping the explosion. Private McGinnis could have easily jumped from the Humvee and saved himself. Instead he dropped inside, put himself against the grenade, and absorbed the blast with his own body.

By that split-second decision, Private McGinnis lost his own life, and he saved his comrades. One of them was Platoon Sergeant Cedric Thomas, who said this: "He had time to jump out of the truck. He chose not to. He's a hero. He was just an awesome guy." For his actions, Private McGinnis received the Silver Star, a posthumous promotion in rank, and a swift nomination for the Medal of Honor. But it wasn't acclaim or credit that motivated him. Ross's dad has said, "I know medals never crossed his mind. He was always about friendships and relationships. He just took that to the ultimate this time."

When Ross McGinnis was in kindergarten, the teacher asked him to draw a picture of what he wanted to be when he grew up. He drew a soldier. Today, our nation recognizing – recognizes him as a soldier, and more than that – because he did far more than his duty. In the words of one of our commanding generals, "Four men are alive because this soldier embodied our Army values and gave his life."

The day will come when the mission he served has been completed and the fighting is over, and freedom and security have prevailed. America will never forget those who came forward to bear the battle. America will always honor the name of this brave soldier who gave all for his country, and was taken to rest at age 19.

I never met PFC McGinnis in person, but I feel honored to know there are still young men and women willing to lay down their life on the altar of freedom. We take for granted the freedoms we have in America. We can lie down and sleep at night in peace because of the men and women who serve to protect our nation against all enemies.

From one vet to another, I thank you.

Chapter 16

Missing Boots

Guiding Principle: Know your values. I mean, really know your values. Then, live your values, regardless of the circumstances.

> *Do not wait for leaders; do it alone, person to person.*
> ~Mother Teresa

In my hand was an envelope addressed to me from the Department of the Army. A million thoughts were going through my head as I opened the letter. They quickly disappeared as I began to read. I could not believe what I was reading. I had been selected to attend Officer Candidate School (OCS)! All of the hard work had paid off. I was heading to Fort Benning, GA for 14 weeks. Upon completion, I would be commissioned as a Second Lieutenant in the U.S. Army. I was one of the 60% that made it through the screening process.

Now let's fast forward several months. It is week 14 of OCS, and it is almost over. We started with over 250 candidates, and we were now down to about 150. We lost the majority of the candidates the very first week. Some simply could not make the cut. Others just did not want to make the cut and quit. After that first week, candidates left OCS for a number of reasons – injuries, failed academics, honor violations, failed PT test, or other requirements (i.e. Land Navigation). This was one of the most challenging things many of us would ever go through. We were pushed beyond the limits of our own understanding. We learned valuable lessons that we will carry with us our entire lives. An entire book can be dedicated to the life lessons and skills we learned. Maybe that will be my next book. For now, I just want to share a few of those lessons.

A couple of things that were grilled in our brain were time management and attention to detail. Everything (and I mean everything) had a place. Not only did it have a place, it was precisely placed. Just so you have an understanding, here are the contents of the middle drawer of your three-drawer chest, and how it should be displayed:

- The middle drawer is opened exactly halfway.
- A towel is folded to cover the entire bottom of the drawer.
- 1 towel. 6 inches wide, neatly rolled, grounded to the left and front of the drawer, and placed so it unrolls to the rear.
- Wash cloth. Folded in quarters, grounded to the left side of drawer and centered between the towel and boot cleaning kit. Smooth fold to the front, double fold to the right.
- Shower Kit. Personal hygiene items for showers, shaving, tooth brush and paste, lotion, etc. This is not to be bulky, dirty, or wet inside. All items are to be clean, neat, and inspectable. Placed to the right

and front of the drawer. The tongue of the zipper to the front of the drawer.
- Boot Cleaning Kit. These items are placed to the rear of the drawer and spaced evenly across the back of the drawer. They are to be clean and appropriate to the types of boots the Officer Candidate has been issued and wears.

So, now you have a very simple idea to the attention to detail that we experienced on a daily basis. As previously mentioned, there are a number of ways in which an Officer Candidate was released from the school. However, the worst and most humiliating way to leave is on an honor violation. An honor violation could consist of, but not limited to, the following: cheating on an exam, stealing, lying, static display, etc. This is where my story starts.

It is week 14, and we have only one other requirement left prior to graduating. We had to complete the 15 mile road march in "full battle rattle" in 3 hours or less. Our platoon had just finished the Dining Facility detail, so we had very little time to get to formation. I ran upstairs, took off my boots, and placed them beside my rucksack. They were part of the packing list, so I needed to make sure they were in the rucksack. Additionally, I would be changing my socks and boots halfway through the march, so I wanted to make sure they were on top. I put on my marching boots and laced them up as quickly as I could. I grabbed my rucksack and ran downstairs to the formation. Shortly after, the road march began.

We reached the halfway point, and I sat down and removed my socks and boots. I opened my rucksack and reached for my boots. That's when a wave of nausea hit me. I emptied everything out of my rucksack, but no boots. In my rush to get to formation, I left them in the room. This was terrible. Following the completion of the road march, we were going to be inspected to ensure we complied with the packing list. Anything missing from the packing list would be considered an unfair advantage and an honor violation. It was the last week of OCS, and I was going to get kicked out because of an honor violation.

This is when insanity kicked in. I began to plot how I could get the boots into the rucksack prior to the inspection. In an effort to shorten the story a bit, I will skip to the end. My plan did not work out. I was caught sneaking into my room to grab my boots. The entire company of Candidates was told that a decision had been made to forego the inspection, until a "certain candidate" was found in contempt of the honor code. The honor code states: "An Officer Candidate will not lie, cheat, or steal, or tolerate those who do." I was ashamed and humiliated. Not only did I bring shame and dishonor upon myself, I let my team down. I waited for several hours to get the order to come downstairs and relieve me from my duty at OCS. For some reason, there was softness in the hearts of the faculty, because instead of getting removed from OCS, I just had to conduct another 15 mile road march the following morning.

The point of the story is that our actions, no matter how small or big, will have an effect on someone other than ourselves. Integrity is at the core of our value system. To be honest with others, I must be honest with myself. My values were not in check that night in OCS when I disobeyed the honor code. If I was completely honest with myself, integrity just had not been one of those core values in my life. Had integrity been a core value in my life at the time, I would not have compromised it, regardless of the outcome.

The good news is that our value system can change. Change is not easy and rarely welcomed, but it is essential. You really cannot judge our book of life by the cover, because each and every one of us live our life from the inside out. Our values tell the story about who we are as a person. They define the personality and the character in each of us. Your values determine how you will react to different situations in life. Some people try to fake their value system, but that will only carry you so far. Eventually, you will be tested, and your true colors will come through. It will happen, because it has happened to me time and time again in my life.

Many times we go through life thinking we know what our values are. They were passed on from our parents, teachers, pastors, coaches, friends, and other family members. Here is the rub in that mentality. Regardless of what we are taught in our life, if we do not believe it, it will not become a "part" of who we are. As an adult, it is our responsibility to mold our children just like we were molded from the time we were born. When we become responsible for our own lives, though, we then become accountable as well. It is then that we need to evaluate our values and see what is truly important in our lives.

In many of my training sessions, I have my students list and define their values. When I say "define," I don't just mean a line or two. I mean at least a paragraph or two. This definition should answer a number of questions:

- What is important to me?
- Why is it important to me?
- Am I living my life in harmony with those values?
- What would I give my life for?
- What do I need to change in my life?

The discovery in this exercise is profound. People have been brought to tears when sharing their definitions. Most realize that their values are probably somewhat different than what they were as kids. How we live our values is a statement of who we are. It is easy to live our values when the seas are calm. It is in the storm where we are tested. It is in those challenging times in our life that we must make a stand. As the lyrics of the song go, "You have to stand for something, or you'll fall for anything." It is what you stand for (or fall for) that tells you and the world the kind of person you have become. If you are not happy with the person you are today, then make a change. Only you can control the outcome of your life. Gandhi said it best: "We must be the change we want to see."

Chapter 17

My Five Minutes of Fame

Guiding Principle: Don't live in the spotlight, but don't fear the spotlight either. For most of us, the spotlight does not happen very often, so it is ok to relish in it for a moment.

> *Let no one ever come to you without leaving better and happier.* ~Mother Teresa

Some of your greatest accomplishments in life will probably be those that you will never know about. I have heard some people say that they are not concerned about leaving a legacy. I don't think you are one of those people, or you would have checked out of this book long before now. The reality is that we are all leaving a legacy. We make a difference in someone's life every day. The question is whether we are making a positive or negative impact. If you glance into your life's rearview mirror and reflect on just yesterday, how many opportunities did you have to make a positive difference in someone's life?

Everyone has a story. Perhaps a smile or a kind greeting could transform an individual's day. That person who accidently bumped into you this morning may have just received some terrible news. The person who cut you off in traffic tonight may have been rushing to make it to his son's last game of the year. Life is frustrating, and we simply do not need additional frustrations. We just need to look for the opportunity to make someone's day. I bet it will be contagious and will affect so many more people than you could ever imagine. You will be a hero in someone's eyes and may not even know it. How cool is that. Here is my Genni story, and I like to believe I am a hero in her eyes. Believing that makes me want to impact even more lives. It's an adrenaline rush.

I was on a plane to Tampa to deliver a speech to a group of sales and marketing folks. I was one of the first ones to board, so I took my normal window seat near the rear of the plane. I settled in and was just gazing out the window, preparing my thoughts as the plane was boarding. The flight attendant announced that it was a completely full flight. So, I did what every person does. As people walked towards the rear of the plane where I was seated, I wondered if they were going to be my companion. Most of the time, I have one of two thoughts going through my mind as I scope the other passengers. The first thought is, "That person does not look so bad. I hope they sit here." The other thought is, "Please God, please God, don't let them sit here." The problem is that everyone else is saying that same prayer. The dilemma is that one person will inevitably not have their prayer answered. However, on this particular flight, I was not sending up any prayers.

The flight was near boarded, and the two seats next to me were still empty. A family of four (dad, mom, and two teenage girls) were heading my way. The girls sat next to me, and the parents sat about four rows back. I said hello to the young lady sitting next to me, and she replied with a simple "Hi." If I had to guess, I would have put her at about 17. The plane took off, and we were on our way. At cruising altitude, she took out her IPOD, and I took out my book. Since I was speaking to sales and marketing folks, I was reading the book I had authored, "Selling at Combat Speed."

About one and one-half hours into the flight, the two sisters start whispering.

"You ask him."

"No, you ask him."

So finally, the girl sitting next to me asked, "Is that a picture of you on the back cover of the book?"

I replied, "Yes it is."

She asked, "Did you write that book?"

Once again, I replied, "Yes."

Then she replied with a voice loud enough for the people two to three rows around us to hear, "Oh my God! I have never met anyone famous, much less sit next to someone famous on a plane! This is so tight!"

I tried to brush it off, saying that it was just a book on sales and not that big of a deal. But she was having nothing of that. She asked, "Do you have another copy?"

I said, "Yes."

Of course, I had a few copies, but I told her that she really would not be very interested in the book. Still, she was persistent. "Would you autograph a book for me?" I agreed and dug through my briefcase to get a new copy of the book. I pulled it out, and she said, "My name is Genni – Genni with a G and Genni with an I." I wrote a small note that said, "Genni, follow your dreams and let your heart be your guide." She was so excited. Then she asked, "Can I get a picture with you? My friends will never believe this." I agreed. She took out her cell phone, gave it to her sister, and leaned over so she could get us both in the shot. "This is so tight," she exclaimed.

So, Genni and I began to talk. I found out she was a senior in high school and just not sure what she wanted to do with her life. She wanted to write, but she did not want to go to college. She always wanted to be an author, but she just assumed that dream only happened to a select few. She asked me all kinds of questions about how to start writing a book, how to get published, how to market the book, and so on. She shared with me that her parents were encouraging her to go to college, but she just wanted to write. She asked me for my advice.

I gave her my advice, which involved going to college. In my mind, I just assumed that she took my advice with a grain of salt and that I was just like another parent. We talked until the plane landed. When it was time for our row to exit, she and her sister slipped over to the adjacent aisle to let me pass so they could wait on their parents. I overheard this conversation: "Mom, look at this picture. See that short guy up there? He wrote a book and signed a copy for me. He is famous. Isn't that tight?"

That was all I heard. It took everything within me to not break out in laughter. I did smile and thought how nice it felt to make someone's day.

Chapter 18

Beat the Bush

Guiding Principle: Stay the course. Even if the finish line is impossible to see, it is probably closer than you think.

> *"Anyone can give up; it's the easiest thing in the world to do. But to hold it together when everyone else would understand if you fell apart, that's true strength."*

It was "Land Navigation" week at Officer Candidate School (OCS). With just a map and a compass, you must maneuver through terrain to find your points with a three hour time limit. During the day, we were expected to find seven of nine points. At night, we had to find two of five points. It was Thursday morning, and it was the first day of solo land navigation. Up until that day, we had gone out in groups. Monday we had groups of six. On Tuesday, we had groups of four. Wednesday, we went out in pairs. All three days, our group had found at least the minimum number of points required to pass the event. It was February in Georgia, but the weather had cooperated. I was feeling quite confident that morning.

The most important part of the land navigation process is the plotting of the points on the map. Grid lines on maps define the coordinate system and are numbered to provide a unique reference. Each point is an 8-digit grid coordinate and is marked with a small dot. Once all points have been plotted, you then determine your route and travel distance between points. I spent about 45 minutes plotting and planning my route that morning. It took me a little less than two hours to find eight of nine points. My confidence continued to grow.

Now, it was Thursday night. You could not ask for better conditions for night land navigation. It was a little brisk, but there was a full moon and no precipitation. Once again, I took about 45 minutes plotting my points. I realized that my first point was very similar to one of the points I had that morning. After spending four days in this terrain, I was starting to become very familiar with it. Here was the concern. To get to my first point, I was going to have to cross a rather deep creek, as well as possibly traverse through what we had called "wait a minute vines." These vines were the homes to thorns that were about one to one and one half inches long.

Due to the depth of the creek and the steepness of the banks, the only way to cross the creek was to find a down tree and walk (scoot) across it. In most cases (probably 99 times out of 100), you are going to have to traverse outside of your azimuth (the direction to the point of interest). Unless it is absolutely necessary, you do not delineate from your azimuth. If you must, there is a method to the madness (I will save you the details). I looked at my map and noticed a much easier route. I could not believe my luck. Instead of going through the woods (beating bush), I could take the dirt road in front of me for about 800 meters. I would then proceed north for 1150 meters. At that exact point, I would shoot a 280 degree azimuth (almost due west) and walk 250 meters to my point. This was going to be a walk in the park!

Prior to "Land Navigation" week, we determined our pace count. We counted the number of paces it took to walk a 100 meter trail through the woods. A pace is determined by leading off with the left foot, and every time the left foot hits the ground, the number incremented by one. My pace count happened to be 67. One of the worst mistakes you can make is not have an accurate pace count. So, we walked this 100 meter trail several times to ensure accuracy. The second worst mistake is to forget how many paces you have gone.

So, off I went. I did not even need my compass. I had a dirt road and a full moon. I found the intersection and turned left. Now I needed to pay special attention to my pace count so I would know exactly where to enter the woods. I picked up 11 rocks and put them in my pocket. After each 67 pace (100 meter) interval, I removed a rock from my pocket. When the last rock was gone, I walked the remaining 33½ paces. Once I arrived, I shot my 280 degree azimuth, picked up two rocks, and started beating bush.

I arrived at my point a few minutes later. The problem was that the sign (similar to a yield sign) was nowhere in sight. I knew my pace count was good, and my azimuth was good. Maybe I just plotted it incorrectly. With an 8-digit grid, it should place me within 10 meters of my point. So, I began to walk around. My point had to be close. I walked in different directions for about five minutes. It was then that I realized I was completely disoriented (notice I did not say lost). I could not remember the direction that I entered the woods. This is where the panic azimuth comes in. If you become disoriented, you could "shoot" a panic azimuth, and that would get you in the direction of the base camp. It was impossible to continue because locating my second point was solely based on finding my first point.

The panic azimuth would have had me beating bush, and I was in no mood for that. So, I shot a backwards azimuth to determine the route back to the dirt road. Once I found the road, I pretty much double timed (ran) back to the base camp hoping I would still have some time left to try again. By the time I arrived back at the camp, there was not enough time for me to go back out. I had failed my first solo night land navigation test. Luckily for me, it was a practice run. However, my confidence began to sway.

I did not sleep well that night. It's difficult enough to sleep on the cold ground with just a sleeping bag and pup tent. Adding in the fact that I was strategizing and planning my actions for the following day made it even more difficult to sleep. It was Friday morning now and test day. We had prepared for this all week. I did not feel prepared at all though. All I could think about was my failure the night before.

For the test, we were using different terrain than what we had practiced on all week. As I previously mentioned, we were becoming increasingly familiar with the practice course. The training needed to prepare us for a real world situation. To accurately critique our skills, we needed to be tested on a course that was completely unfamiliar to us. Train as you fight!

I passed the daytime land navigation exercise with flying colors, finding eight of nine points. My confidence was still shaken though. As the afternoon approached, the clouds started rolling in. Night fell, and the moon was hidden behind the clouds. I plotted my points and took off. Tonight, the dirt road option never even crossed my mind. I was beating bush! My first point was only about 900 meters away. A little over 100 meters into the woods, the rain began to fall. I could not believe it. Could it get any worse? (Have you ever noticed when you ask that question that it normally seems to get worse?)

Around the 400 meter point, I approached a creek. Do you think there was a downed tree for me to cross? Of course not. So I walked left for 67 paces. No tree. I walked right 100 paces to get back to my starting point. Then I continued walking (and praying). About 42 paces later, my prayers were answered – a tree. Normally, I would have walked across the tree, but the rain made the barkless tree extremely slippery. So, I scooted. I made it to the other side and walked back 42 paces to my starting location. Several minutes later, I arrived at my first point. I did a fist pump and a short victory dance. My confidence meter began to peg once again.

My second point was the longest of the five – 1300 meters. I took off feeling good about the final results. About 700 meters into my second point, it happened. I ran into a wall of the "wait a minute" vines. We should have nicknamed them "wait an hour" vines. I did not know how wide this wall of vines was, and I had no intention in straying from my azimuth. So, I headed straight into the vines. The cuts and gashes would heal. I could not afford to fail this exercise.

After about 10 minutes, I was still in this wall of vines. I began to get discouraged. The exposed areas of my body (hands and face) were scratched. The blood mixed with the rain, so I had no idea the extent of my wounds. After another five minutes, I made the decision that I should look for an alternate exit point. I took out my red lens flashlight, which provides little visibility even in the best of conditions. I looked in front of me. I looked to my left, and then to my right. There was no way in "you know what" that I was going back in the direction I came. Everywhere I looked, there was a wall of thorny vines. I could have gone left or right as an option, but I made the decision to continue straight forward.

About five minutes later, I stepped out of grasp of the "wait a minute" vines. I looked at my watch and noticed that I had spent about 35 minutes traversing them. Obviously, my pace count was skewed, so I went on a best-guess estimate on how far I had gone. My guess was about 20 meters (13½ paces). I ended up finding my second point. As a matter of fact, I found four of the five points.

There are many lessons that can be learned. Here are a few:

- Have a plan. Know where you are going and how long it will take to get there.
- You will have some rainy days. Plan for it.
- Team work is vital to our success – personal and professional.
- The easy road is probably not the best road. Remember the words of Robert Frost: "I took the road less traveled, and that has made all the difference."
- Obstacles are a part of life. The best course of action is to handle them head on. If you try to avoid them, you risk losing your way.
- Reaching your destination builds confidence. The journey builds character.
- Plan to fail, but learn from your failures.
- Hard work, determination, and courage will often prevail over a lack of confidence.

Chapter 19

My Hero

Guiding Principle: We all need a hero in our lives. If you don't have one, look around. You may be surprised by who winds up being your hero.

> *A hero is no braver than an ordinary man, but he is braver five minutes longer.* ~Ralph Waldo Emerson

As you start reading this chapter, you are probably thinking it has a biased slant. That's one of the reasons why it is near the back of the book, as opposed to the front. I did not want to send the wrong first impression. However, since I am the author, I get to write whatever I choose. This chapter is about my hero – my son. His name is Michael, but because of all the Michaels we have in the house (as I mentioned in a previous chapter), I will refer to him as Mike Jr. Most of the time, he is just Jr. His life was not a bed of roses either. He bears both the physical and emotional scars, yet he always seems to overcome adversity and learn valuable life lessons. I won't go into much detail about his life, because I want this chapter to be written from his point of view. However, I do need to preface it with a little background information.

Mike Jr. was an army brat. For those who do not know what that is, an army brat is the term given to dependent children of a parent serving in the military. He was born in Germany. One month after he was born, I was sent to Iraq to fight the first Gulf War. I missed the first six months of his life. When he was three years old, I left for 114 days to attend Officer Candidate School. When he was four years old, I deployed to Guantanamo Bay, Cuba for three months.

Between the ages of five and nine, I was deployed on numerous training exercises ranging from a couple of days to six weeks at a time. My focus was my military career. When Mike Jr. turned nine, his mother and I divorced. Since I was still in the Army, we saw each other even less. Even when I was "there," I really wasn't "there." So, technically, he spent most of his childhood without me being in his life. To this day, I do not understand how we could be as close as we are. I always said we were "best buds," and I still believe that is the case, even though the miles have separated us.

However, I have to believe that Mike Jr.'s greatest loss is that of his sister. One of the most difficult questions for a bereaved parent to answer is, "How many children do you have?" Equally difficult for the sibling is, "How many brothers and sisters do you have?" You see, the surviving sibling is probably one of the most difficult roles a child could ever be placed into. They are the "forgotten" griever. They can see the visible pain their parents have after the loss of a child. So they hide their grief so they can be strong for their parents. So, I asked Mike Jr. to describe in his own words how this horrific accident that took his sister's life and left him both physically and emotionally injured affected his life. I did not change the words or the content, so I apologize if any words or phrases offend anyone. Here are his words:

I pretty much remember everything that I was awake for. The first thing I remember is just driving down the road and beginning to swerve. We swerved a hard right, then left, then went to swerve right again (and I heard mom say Scheiße – which I knew meant "shit" in German), and that's when we hit. I did not get knocked unconscious. As soon as we hit, the first thing I noticed was the intense smell that I had never smelled before. I know now that it was the smell of the airbag. My face was pretty much numb and felt swollen. I looked over at my mom, and she looked like something in a cartoon. Her hands were on the wheel, and her head was moving in a small circle while she moaned. Our dog, Major, obviously did not get knocked out either because I could hear him yelping like crazy. The next thing I saw is probably the image that I will always remember most in my life. I looked in the back seat and saw Maci. She was sitting normal, and her eyes were wide and staring straight into mine as if she had just seen a ghost. Sometimes I wonder if maybe I was one of the last people to ever see her eyes open. I turned back around and started looking around. Then survival mode came into effect. I went to unbuckle my seat belt, but I couldn't. I looked down and saw my wrist hanging on by my skin. I figured out later that it could just move back and forth without bending, because I remember looking at it again later, and it was in the right place. I looked at my mom again, took the back of my hand, and rubbed it up against her right forearm, and said "I love you." I remember it sounded pretty bad because my face was pretty messed up, kind of like I was saying it without using my tongue. Then I looked out my window at the car next to us. A woman was in her car with the window rolled down and shouted, "Are you ok?" That's when I said "help" as best I could. The next thing I remember, the woman is at the window saying that she was going to leave me in the car until the ambulance arrived. There is a little space between the open hood and the car where you can see in front of you; it is probably about three or four inches wide. Through this little space, I saw a flame burst up. That is when I heard the woman mutter something, and she quickly pulled me through the window. She ran me a good distance and laid me down on the road. That's when I told her to go back for mom and Maci.

I don't know how much time had passed, but apparently the shock was wearing off because I began to experience excruciating pain for the first time since the collision. The next thing I remember, I was being put into the ambulance. I stayed awake for a little while because I remember the guys trying to keep me awake by asking stupid questions. I didn't realize it was important for me to stay awake since I was in shock, so I was getting kind of annoyed when I was being asked the same couple of questions over and over again. I guess eventually I did end up falling asleep though because I don't remember arriving at the hospital and being moved and all that stuff. The next memory I even have from this point is waking up and seeing a couple of my mom's friends. I also remember waking up periodically and hearing the person next to me watching Sponge Bob Square Pants. I don't know how long I had to stay on that hard bed, but I remember asking about mom and Maci, and you (Dad) trying to tell me that Maci had not made it, but you broke into tears. I can't remember if you completed the statement, or if someone else had to step in. I'm thinking it might have been the latter. That news put me straight into shock again. I don't remember crying at that moment, probably because I wasn't in the right state of mind, but it definitely hit me hard. I felt like it was one of those things that you feel like could never happen to you; like it was saved for someone else, but then you found out that you are actually that "someone else."

I think everyone has different ways to cope with hard things like this. I found out that for me, the only thing that helped was time and being around family members and close friends. I remember my mom having me go to some kind of grieving camp for a couple days because she thought it would help. I absolutely hated it. One thing I do remember that kind of was weird though was that we had to make a pillow. I had a shirt that was Maci's that I was going to cut and sew onto the pillow. When I pulled the shirt out, it smelled like her. I really don't remember how I felt about that though.

I know people grieve differently. For me, personally, I did not like to express my feelings around other people, and I didn't like to get into emotional conversations about the subject. I mourned on my own time and just have my own personal time to recollect. A lot of times, this often led to crying in bed when I was trying to sleep. But that's just me. I've never really been the emotional, mushy kind of guy.

As a result of my injuries, I was forced to use a wheelchair for mobility. I have always been active, and being confined to the wheelchair was probably more agonizing than the physical pain. I often made my mom mad when she found out I had been outside playing basketball. The wheelchair was on the basketball court; I was just not in it. I think this is where I developed the mentality that went a little like this: "If it's not hurting me, then I'm not going to pay attention to it." Sometimes this is a bad mentality to have, but whatever. I know my physical limits. It also made me learn that even the worst of injuries will heal eventually. As time passed, I would also learn that physical pain heals much quicker than the emotional pain. I would also learn that the emotional scars run much deeper than the physical scars.

Like I said, though, time heals everything. It sucks, but you have to keep on pushing through it. I think it was a little harder in our case because we lost someone in the blink of an eye and didn't have time to prepare ourselves (such as the time that a person has when they realize that their loved one is going to eventually die of cancer).

I know how difficult it was for Mike Jr. to write these words because I, myself, had to revisit the memory of that time and allow old emotional wounds to be reopened when writing Maci's Place. Although Mike Jr. says that time heals everything, I would have to expound a little more on that phrase. A parent never heals from losing a child. I have to believe the same about a sibling. What time does though is to help that pain be less intense. Eventually, we all learn to live with our losses, but our life after that loss is much different than life before the loss.

As I read these words that my son wrote, my heart was consumed by this overwhelming pain. Because his grieving style is so much like mine, we never really sat down and talked about the accident in great detail. I was so proud when he shared his raw emotions with me, even if it was in writing. Just when I thought I could not be more proud of him, he goes and proves me wrong. I asked him what lessons he learned from this experience, and his response filled my heart with overwhelming pride. Here was his response:

I think everyone is different when it comes to coping. Even if someone experienced the exact situation I did, I don't think there is really much you could say to make them feel better. At times like those, you cannot get your mind off of what has happened, no matter what anyone says. The only thing that I would tell them would be that it may not look like it, but things will get better. It will become a little easier to accept day by day, until finally it is to the point where you feel like you have met closure. There were a couple of things that people did that really made an impact on me personally. One thing was obviously my dad. The first few nights when I was experiencing the physical pain in recovering, he stayed by my bedside. I was hooked up to an IV and was given a "clicker" to control my dosage of morphine. The nurse said it could be clicked every 20 minutes to help control the pain. The only time I was really waking up was when the pain was so intense that it woke me from a dead sleep. My dad has been through several surgeries and knows it is more difficult to play catch-up to pain control than to manage the pain. So, he stayed awake and clicked the button every 20 minutes.

Another thing that helped me was when people came to visit me. I know many people visited, but it is my friends that I remember the most. It is times like this when you realize who your true friends are.

I definitely have more compassion towards others who have lost loved ones because it is more personal to me; I know how they feel. It is a pain that cannot be imagined, only experienced. After looking back on the accident, I feel like I am a lot more mentally tough as well. I feel like if I made it through that, then I can do anything, which goes hand in hand with my drive to push myself to new heights, such as the Army. It made me realize that life is a gift that can be taken away from you at any moment. One of my favorite quotes now is: "If you're not living on the edge, you're taking up too much space." I want to experience everything that life has to offer, and I refuse to let anything hold me back. I have the drive to push forward and challenge myself to go above and beyond in every-thing that I do.

I have been through a lot at a young age. It has taught me one important thing: life goes on. It is not the end of the world if something terrible happens to you. There are some people that are willing to take their own life to get rid of pain. This is not the route to take. That means you have given up. You have given up on others, and you have given up on yourself. From what I have been through, I know that I will be able to overcome any obstacle that may present itself, whether it be physical or emotional. I have learned that you have to believe in order to achieve. If you don't believe in yourself, then how do you expect others to? Bad things that happen in your life are just tests designed to test your willpower to keep on truckin'. If you can get through the difficult times, then the times that are not as hard will be a breeze. I think that is why I have such a desire to strive for the best at whatever I do, because times are not hard for me. Times are not hard, so let's throw some difficulty in my life that will only benefit me and make me better. My past experiences have made me stronger. The saying is true, "What doesn't kill you will only make you stronger." I am a living example and will cherish my life.

Son, I am so proud of the man you have become. Thank you for always believing in me. You truly are my hero!

After reading this, you have to be thinking to yourself, "Now that is an incredible young man." If you are a teenager or young adult and going through a difficult time, I hope Mike Jr.'s story will provide hope and encouragement. He does live life to the fullest. We both do. Just in the past couple of years, we have both purchased a motorcycle and gone sky diving. Yeah, we push the envelope and live life on the edge. That's just what we do!

Chapter 20

Mix-Matched Socks

**Guiding Principle: Don't pole vault over mouse turds.
(In other words, don't sweat the small stuff or don't
make a mountain out of a mole hill.)**

> *If you have time to whine and complain about something,
> then you have the time to do something about it.*
> ~Anthony J. D'Angelo

I believe that when you make changes in your personal life, it transfers over into your professional life as well. The same holds true for the changes we make in our professional life. It transfers over into your personal life. Why? Because you are not changing behaviors, you are changing your mentality. When you change, you are changing. Duh! What I am trying to say is that change is a holistic approach. If you change a small part of your life, it will affect your entire life. Cool huh?

Up to this point, the book has focused on your "strong finish" in your personal life. I want to shift gears and focus on a small part of the professional aspect. Your success will depend upon the relationships you have in your life. To quote Allan C. Emery, "If you see a turtle on the fencepost, you can guarantee it did not get there by itself." So look for opportunities to place people in your life who have your best interest in mind.

It was a routine trip. I was scheduled to deliver a keynote presentation. I would fly in, speak, and fly back out the same day. It would be a quick flight. I woke up early and arrived at the airport two hours early like normal. Does anybody else still arrive at the airport two hours early? Were you ever in the military? We military folks are anal retentive about being on time. I don't think we ever get it out of our blood. I find that I am in a hurry even when I am not in a hurry!

If you are not in the military and have never been in the military, but you still have to arrive two hours early, you should go enlist. You would make a fine soldier. Arriving two hours early just does not fit into the personality traits of a normal corporate America business person.

So, my flight was scheduled to leave at 7:30 A.M. I arrived around 5:30 A.M., breezed through security, and was at my gate before 6:00 A.M. That's the story of my life. My wife says I am nuts. But back in 1992, I arrived at the airport to find the computers down. They were processing every boarding pass by hand, and it took me one and one-half hours just to get my boarding pass. I did not miss my plane because everyone else was in the same situation. However, that did not keep me from sweating bullets. So, even though it has been 17 years since that incident, and you can now check in and print boarding passes online, I remain scarred for life.

So, I was at the gate. I pulled out a book and started reading to pass time. About five minutes into the book, this woman sat down next to me.

"Good morning, ma'am."

"Good morning young man."

I went back to reading, but I was not really reading. The entire gate area was practically empty, and I was wondering why she had chosen to sit next to me even though there were so many open seats. After about seven and one-half seconds, the thought left me, and I began actually reading. After about 10 minutes of reading and several "crossovers" later (crossovers being the shift in your body weight and the crossing over your legs), I felt this nudge.

"Young man, do you realize your socks don't match?" Those are words that strike terror in the heart of the anal retentive soldier types. So, I did what any normal person would have done. I had to see for myself as if she would have some hidden agenda about lying about my mix-matched socks. She was right. But I have to be honest with you, only the trained eye could have spotted that mistake. I had one black sock and one dark navy blue sock, but they both had the same patterns. This had happened before. It is very easy to confuse the color of socks if you are in the wrong light. I started thinking to myself, "How long had she actually been staring at my socks? She could only see one sock at a time as I performed my crossover. I was getting a little nervous. Maybe she was a stalker?" Ok that was the ego talking.

So, while I was performing a recon on my socks, I started replaying the events of the night before and analyzing how this could have happened. It did not take long for me to figure out how this had happened. Allow me to paint you a picture that many of you can probably relate to.

I have two boys at home – 12 and 15 years old. They are true Generation Y kids. So, the night before I was leaving, the last load of clothes was being washed as I packed. I heard the dryer buzz, so I went into the living room to tell the boys to get the clothes out of the dryer and start folding. This was the scene. The television was on. They both had their laptops on and doing "God only knows what." I could hear the music blasting from the headphones that were connected to their IPODS. And they both had their cell phones sitting beside them, occasionally vibrating when a new text message came in. Ok, let's go over that list again – television, laptop, IPOD, and cell phone. They had no earthly idea that I walked into the room. At that moment, I was not sure if they even knew I existed. They were in their own Generation Y world. So, I put my fingers in my mouth and let out this high pitch whistle. I think it woke up all the neighborhood dogs. The normal person would have jumped out of their skin. (I believe my wife who was in the other room and actually did). However, the boys nonchalantly lifted their heads with this look on their face. It was a "I think I may have heard an odd noise, but I am not sure" look. All of a sudden, I was noticed.

"What up?"

"Guys, the final load of clothes are done. I need you to sort the socks and make sure you keep a pair of my black socks out for my trip. If you work together, it should only take you about 10 minutes, and then you can go back to your business."

I came back after about 20 minutes later. They were sitting on the couch with a pile of socks between them. Both of them were watching TV and texting. They had about four pairs of socks done. I was not in a big hurry, but just to keep them on task, I said, "Come on boys, let's get moving."

They replied, "Ok, we are almost done." <Yeah Right>

So, eventually they finished the laundry and put the socks away, except for my pair of black socks that were folded together (one inside the other) and lying beside my shoes. I was ready to go.

So, there I sat, trying to come up with a good reason to tell this lady why I had on mix-matched socks. She must have seen the look of terror on my face and said, "Don't worry. It's hardly noticeable." I thought, "How kind of her to lie to me."

So, I began to tell her how this all happened. She thought the story was hilarious and was cracking up. Her laughter was contagious, and I began to laugh it off as well. The next thing you know, we were sharing pictures of our family. Before we knew it, it was time to board. We were flying Southwest, and as you know, it is open seating. I had enjoyed our conversation so much that I invited her to sit with me on the plane. She accepted.

We talked the entire flight to California. We talked about kids, spouses, religion, politics, business, and even a little sports. Upon exiting the plane, we exchanged business cards and went our separate ways. I went to the hotel, gave my speech, and nobody mentioned my socks.

A few weeks later, I received a small package in the mail from Los Angeles. I opened the package to find two pairs of brand new socks and a note. The note read:

> *"Mike, I just wanted to thank you for sharing your stories with me. They really made a difference in my life. Your stories made me realize that I have the power to make something good out of a bad situation. I can't believe my life has been impacted by a pair of mix-matched socks. Take these socks as a token of my appreciation. If all it takes is a pair of mix-matched socks to change a person's life, consider this my contribution. Thank you for making a difference in my life."*
>
> *Your Changed Friend, Holly.*
>
> *P.S. Call me on Monday. I want to learn more about your business.*

Holly's company was one of the largest accounts we have closed. And every year at Christmas, I receive a pair of socks.

Conclusion

A couple of years ago, I was flying to Tampa for business. Like normal, I decided to strike up a conversation with the lady sitting next to me. We talked for a few hours, but one thing she said in particular seemed to stick with me. She had lived in Phoenix most of her adult life. She was 50 years old and heading back to Tampa to open a bed and breakfast. She said, "When you are 50 years old and your kids are in college, it's time to start thinking about enjoying the rest of your life."

The unfortunate truth is that most of us are not doing what really makes us happy. We do what we can to make ends meet, and then worry about being happy later in our life. We always expect there will be a "later" for us. The fortunate ones figure out earlier than the others that we should not have to settle. It is up to us to make our dreams come true.

On a flight back in 2002, for some reason I had decided to take an aisle seat. It was going to be about a five hour flight, and we were going to arrive very late that night. It was a few hours into the flight, and I thought the majority of the passengers had fallen asleep. The passengers sitting in my row had been snoozing for quite some time. The cabin lights had been dimmed, I could not hear any chatter from around me, and the flight attendants had not passed by in quite some time. I had my book in my hand, but apparently had stopped reading and was lost in thought. That's when I heard his voice.

"You seem to have a lot on your mind, young man. You have not turned the page of that book in about 20 minutes. For a second, I thought you might be sleeping." I turned around to get a look at the guy who had started the conversation. He was an elderly man, and even though the lights had been dimmed, I could see he was in amazing shape. Although the features of his face had been hardened through the years, he had a gentleness in his eyes that just seemed to put me at ease.

"Well, I had every intention of reading to pass along the time, but I guess I did kind of get lost in my thoughts." And so the conversation began. His name was Stewart, but his friends called him Stu. The comfort of sharing stories and experiences was as if we had known each other our entire lives. He had some amazing stories to tell, and had anyone else been listening, they would have drawn the same conclusion: This man has made his fortune and has experienced all that life has to offer. He never came across as boasting. You just knew from the stories he told. He was fascinating, and I was hanging onto every word.

We probably talked for about an hour when he said he was going to try to get some rest. I told him it was a pleasure meeting him. What happened next is what eventually changed my life. It had been about a year since my daughter had passed, but that never came up in conversation. As a matter of fact, this was the first time in a very long time that I could actually enjoy a lengthy conversation with someone. After the car accident, I had pushed everyone out of my life. He had no idea what was going on in my life. Neither of us could have known what I would put myself through that year in the name of grief. However, he must have sensed something in my life.

Just before he closed his eyes, he asked me, "Mike, how old do you think I am?"

Now, I am terrible with that question. I am amazed how people at amusement parks and fairs are so good at guessing other people's age. I am always worried that I might offend someone by giving my true opinion. For some reason though, I did not feel like I would offend him. "Well Stewart…"

He interrupted me and said, "Mike, call me Stu. All my friends call me Stu."

So, I continued. "Well, Stu, I am not very good at the age-guessing game. I hope I don't offend you, but I would have to guess around 65-70ish." Stu began to chuckle. Then he said:

"Mike, I am 83 years old. I am in amazing shape and have no real medical issues. I have travelled the world and have made, lost, and remade fortunes. I have had amazing friends and was blessed to have married my best friend. Living this long is both a blessing and a curse. I am healthy and get to enjoy living my life to the fullest. However, the curse is that I have outlived my wife, two of my children, and many of my lifelong friends.

I worked hard, and played even harder. I have enjoyed the finer things in life. If I had to go back and do things over, I would not change a thing. My life has been so good, there are times when I look around and feel a sense of guilt as others around me struggle day to day. Not to boast, but I have given hundreds of thousands of dollars and countless hours of my time to charities and other organizations around the world. God has truly blessed me.

I have had a great life, but my best is yet to come. Mike, no matter where you are in your life or whatever you are going through, keep your focus on God and the things that are important in your life. Your best is yet to come."

With that, Stu closed his eyes and went to sleep. When the plane landed, we exchanged farewells and went our separate ways. Although I was still in a major funk in my life and would be for another year, it was those words from Stu that have encouraged me over the years.

Today is a new day. Today the book of your life has a blank page in it, one that you can fill with anything that suits you. You could spend today in bed, hiding under the blankets, at work buried in your work, or spend it with your family, sitting at the dinner table talking about....anything.

Each day is a new day, a new beginning, and a new opportunity. No matter what you are facing today, there are, and always will be, other opportunities for you to do more with your own life. You cannot change what has happened in the past, nor can you overlook the changes it has made in your day-to-day life. Perhaps you are forever altered; someone different and mangled from where you used to be. Yet you can find a tomorrow with a new page waiting to be written.

There are no experts that can tell you when the pain will stop. There is no answer to the question, "Why?" You may never come to a definite place of understanding, but you can get to a place in your life where you make a difference.

Tomorrow starts anew, a new day, and a new blank page. You can do anything with that day. How will you spend your day? In sorrow or in love with the plan God has in store for you. Will you spend your day with a bottle of liquor in hand, hoping to make the pain go away? Will you take the next step of forgiveness for yourself, your God, your family, and friends?

In your book, there are chapters that define your life. These chapters have been written and cannot be changed. However, your book does not stop there. Your book is full of blank pages for tomorrow. Fill those pages in the way that will make a difference in someone's life.

Remember, God is not finished with you just yet. God has work for you to do and lessons for you to learn. He has a plan in your life. It does not matter what you did in the past. The only thing that matters is what you do right now. Will you put this book aside and let it collect dust, or will you make a commitment to yourself to begin your "strong finish" right now? No matter where you are in your life journey or what you are going through right this very minute, your best is yet to come. Remember, today is the first day of the rest of your life. Make a difference now!

If I Had My Life to Live Over by Erma Bombeck

- I would have invited friends over to dinner, even if the carpet was stained and the sofa faded.
- I would have eaten the popcorn in the GOOD living room and worried much less about the dirt when someone wanted to light a fire in the fireplace.
- I would have taken the time to listen to my grand-father ramble about his youth.
- I would never have insisted the car windows be rolled up on a summer day because my hair had just been teased and sprayed.
- I would have burned the pink candle sculpted like a rose before it melted in storage.
- I would have sat on the lawn with my children and not worried about grass stains.
- I would have cried and laughed less while watching television, and more while watching life.
- I would have gone to bed when I was sick instead of pretending the earth would go into a holding pattern if I wasn't there for the day.
- I would never have bought anything just because it was practical, wouldn't show soil, or was guaranteed to last a lifetime.
- Instead of wishing away nine months of pregnancy, I'd have cherished every moment, realizing that the wonderment growing inside me was the only chance in life to assist God in a miracle.
- When my kids kissed me impetuously, I would never have said, "Later. Now go get washed up for dinner."
- There would have been more "I love you's" and more "I'm sorry's," but mostly, given another shot at life, I would seize every minute.....look at it and really see it...live it. And never give it back.

Guiding Principles

Chapter 1 – Guiding Principle: "Today is the first day of the rest of your life. Make a difference now."

Chapter 2 – Guiding Principle: Things may appear dismal at best. You may feel like no one has ever suffered like you are now. Look around you though. Someone will have it worse than you. Healing comes in taking the focus off of you and placing it on someone else.

Chapter 3 – Guiding Principle: Occasionally glance into life's rearview mirror as a reminder of lessons learned. Spend the majority of your time looking ahead.

Chapter 4 – Guiding Principle: Making the choice is the easy part. Acting on that choice takes courage.

Chapter 5 – Guiding Principle: If you say you will deliver, you better be the world's best mailman.

Chapter 6 – Guiding Principle: Put some legs on your dreams.

Chapter 7 – Guiding Principle: Some days you are the dog, and other days you are the fire hydrant. When you get the opportunity, be ready to choose. Don't let the choice be made for you.

Chapter 8 – Guiding Principle: Be a generous giver – not because you reap what you sow, but because it just feels good!

Chapter 9 – Guiding Principle: Showing up is the easy part. Earning the right to be heard is the challenge.

Chapter 10 – Guiding Principle: Talent will only take you so far. Then you will need to depend upon your heart to kick in and take over.

Chapter 11 – Guiding Principle: Life has a way of teaching us huge lessons. It's the little things that make such a major difference. Look for ways to make an impact on another life.

Chapter 12 – Guiding Principle: A small thank you means more than you can possibly imagine.

Chapter 13 – Guiding Principle: Sometimes the life you think you are saving is actually saving your life.

Chapter 14 – Guiding Principle: You do not have to be a celebrity or someone famous to make an impact. You just have to be willing.

Chapter 15 – Guiding Principle: If you love your freedom, thank a vet.

Chapter 16 – Guiding Principle: Know your values. I mean, really know your values. Then, live your values regardless of the circumstances.

Chapter 17 – Guiding Principle: Don't live in the spotlight, but don't fear the spotlight either. For most of us, the spotlight does not happen very often, so it is ok to relish in it for a moment.

Chapter 18 – Guiding Principle: Stay the course. Even if the finish line is impossible to see, it is probably closer than you think.

Chapter 19 – Guiding Principle: We all need a hero in our lives. If you don't have one, look around. You may be surprised by who winds up being your hero.

Chapter 20 – Guiding Principle: Don't pole vault over mouse turds. (In other words, don't sweat the small stuff or don't make a mountain out of a mole hill.)